Santa says -

" Experience The Christmas

spirit every day '

Grover C. Gorbee

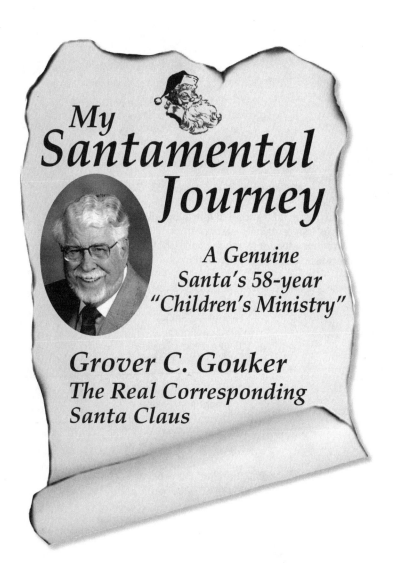

My
Santamental
Journey

A Genuine
Santa's 58-year
"Children's Ministry"

Grover C. Gouker
The Real Corresponding
Santa Claus

My Santamental Journey
A Genuine Santa's 58-year "Children's Ministry"
Grover C. Gouker, The Real Corresponding Santa Claus
Cover Design by Sharon Martin, The Wright Impression

Published by Grover C. Gouker
Lancaster, Pennsylvania

Published by

Grover C. Gouker
gouker.com
105 Greenview Drive
Lancaster, PA 17601

Design and layout
The Wright Impression
wrightimpression.com
54 Witmer Road
Conestoga, PA 17516

International Standard Book Number (ISBN)
978-0-615-20260-0

Printed in the United States of America
1st printing

About the Author

Grover C. Gouker

Grover C. Gouker is a semi-retired, nationally known Public Speaker, Motivator and Humorist. He taught his own courses in Human Relations and People Skills, Sales, and Public Speaking. Grover has conducted thousands of workshops, seminars, and presentations for business, organizations, civic groups, conventions, hospitals and educational groups. He has spoken to more than 20,000 audiences. Grover is often referred to as the "William Jennings Bryan of the Jaycees." He refers to himself as the Professor of Common Sense, Ongoing Student in the University of Life.

As a community leader, he is a Former President of the Hanover Jaycees, State President of the Pennsylvania Jaycees and Vice-President of the U.S. Jaycees, Founder of the Hanover Area YMCA, Founder of the Hanover Friends of the Library and Former President of the Kiwanis Club in Hanover. He is a Former Chapter Chairman of the American Red Cross and Former Founder and Commander of the AMVETS in his hometown of Hanover, Pennsylvania. He was elected to the World President's Committee on Community Development–Junior Chamber International. The Korean Ambassador cited Grover for special recognition for the State Chairmanship of Korean War Orphans. He was inducted into the United States Junior Chamber of Commerce Leadership Hall of Fame in 2004 and was awarded the prestigious Jefferson Award in 2005 for community service.

His most treasured avocation is his "Letters to Santa" project, which has entitled him to the name of "Official Corresponding Santa Claus." Grover and his 58-year project were featured on ABC on Ted Koppel's Nightline on Christmas Eve, 2001.

Grover lives in Lancaster, Pennsylvania, with his wife, Gloria.

Dedication

This book is dedicated to my late wife, Mary Louise, my two lovely daughters, Patti and Peg, my only dear granddaughter, Erin, and my beautiful caring wife, Gloria. All of these people, in some small part, or in some cases, in large measure, have assisted me in my journey of joy over the past 58 years as the "Official Corresponding Santa Claus." I also would like to dedicate this book to the more than 100,000 children and adults who have written to me over the past 58 years, from seven different countries and all of our 50 states.

Mary Louise Gouker

Patti S. Ensminger

Peggy J. Kyle

Erin N. Kyle

Gloria J. Gouker

Acknowledgements

To Gloria, my beautiful wife, who is always by my side and in my corner—You are my true inspiration. You knew how important this dream book was to me and your patience and months and months of typing, editing and organizing is so much appreciated. Side by side and always as a team, we have spread sunshine and smiles to "little believers" and "big believers" all over the world. Everyone expects Mrs. Santa to be nice and you are just SANTASTIC! Thank you, my love.

To Patti, my daughter who urged me to put this dream project into a book. Finally, because of your encouragement, it is now a reality. I appreciate your confidence and belief in me, as well as your financial support in making this happen. I love you, Patti.

To Peg, my daughter who is the reason I can continue this project. With the very busy life you live, you have always managed to take the time to answer the letters that are dropped off at the log cabin in Center Square in Hanover. I know this takes extra effort and I am so thankful to have a loyal daughter like you who is truly a real-life Brownie. I love you, Peg.

To Erin, my one and only granddaughter. You are such a fine example of what young people should be today. Thank you for being such a terrific granddaughter and helping me to keep my youthful thoughts. I am so proud of you and I love you, Erin.

When I moved from Hanover to Lancaster, the Hanover Post Office went the extra mile by forwarding to me collections of letters that came into their post office addressed to Santa Claus. To this day, more than 34 years later, they still take special effort to continue this process so children will get their own individualized letters.

Although this project has been self-funded through the years, I would be remiss if I didn't express my sincerest gratitude to the Hanover Jaycees who have made contributions toward my postage over the years. Keep in mind that when I first started answering letters from Santa Claus, it cost only three cents a letter!

To all the friends, acquaintances and people I will never know—Thank you so much for enclosing, along with the child's letter, anywhere from a single stamp to a complete book of stamps. I never ask for this generous gift; however, I know the true Spirit of Giving prompted you to do this nice gesture.

My genuine thanks to Cheryl Broad, RN/RAc, who introduced me to her friend, Sharon Martin, owner of The Wright Impression. Sharon is a bright, exciting, enthusiastic graphic designer and marketing specialist who helped me tremendously, and always with a smile on her face. What a treasure! Sharon was my compass on this *Santamental Journey.* It was a great trip, wasn't it, Sharon?

My sincere thanks to Jodi Arthur whose professional editing guidance proved invaluable. And, special thanks to Monique Anton, owner of Launch Marketing, for her honest evaluation and expertise.

Preface

Time is precious to all of us and we don't always take time for the most important people in our lives—our children. This collection of Santa letters will remind you of the innocent love and laughter that children share so easily. If you want to stop for a moment to remember what it was like to be a child who has dreams and fantasies, perhaps you will be able to read this book and reawaken that part of you.

Contents

Chapter One
The World is Alive with the "Sound of Laughter"

"Boy, I feel good!" Those are the words I choose to say every morning as I start my day. That's one of my choices. Another of my choices is to find humor in life's happenings. After all, laughter is a great stress reliever. I've even heard it described as "inside jogging" because it helps release endorphins.

For me, one of the greatest sources of joy and humor over the last 58 years has been reading and responding to children's letters to Santa as a real corresponding Santa Claus. While some of the letters are poignant and touching, such as those written after the terror attacks on Sept. 11, most are created with a childlike innocence that never ceases to amuse and amaze me.

In the pages that follow, I'd like to share some of my favorite letters with you in the hope of tickling your funny bone and awakening the childlike spirit inside of you. I hope you enjoy them as much as I do.

Presents Aren't Everything

For some children, writing to Santa isn't about asking for presents. Sometimes they just have something they want to say. Take Bobby, Amy and Kyle for example.

"Dear Santa,
I don't know what I want. I just got over a cold. I ate nine
or 10 oranges. I am learning to play the piano and I hate it.
Love, Bobby"

"Dear Santa,
I'm pretty busy and I guess you're pretty busy too.
I'm 8 years old and I'm 44 inches long.
Love, Amy."

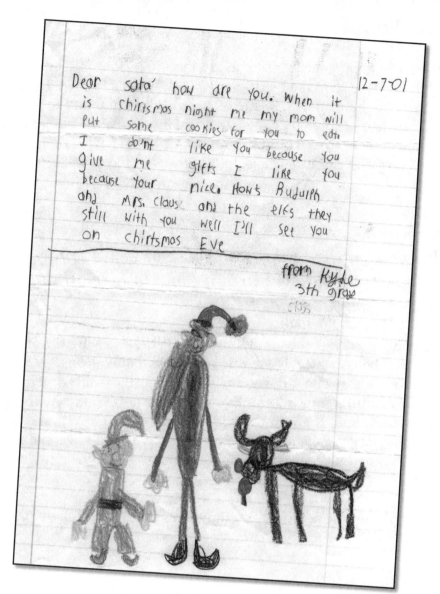

"*Dear Santa,*

How are you. When it is Chirstmas night me my mom will put some cookies for you to eat. I don't like you because you give me gifts I like you because your nice. How's Rudulph and Mrs. Claus and the elfs they still with you well I'll see you on Chirtsmas Eve
from Kyle
3th grade"

Not one of them ever asked for a blessed thing. You see, what they're going to get is not all that important to these kids. They have something on their minds and they know Santa Claus can relate to it. Maybe their parents can't, but Santa Claus can.

Positive About Negativity

I'd like to tell you about a little girl named Mary Beth from Pittsburgh, Pennsylvania, who also felt the need to make her thoughts and feelings known. It would be fair to say that Mary Beth had a negative streak. It's okay to say that. I'm a very positive person, but I'm also positive that she had a negative streak! And her letters always revealed it somewhere. You would think she would have been on her best behavior when she was writing to Santa Claus, but that wasn't the case, as you can see in the following letter.

> *"Dear Santa,*
> *I'll bet you get tired taking all those presents to the good kids. I know I would get tired if I had to take all those presents to the good kids."*

She had something against the good kids, didn't she? Mary Beth went on to say, *"I got a cold because Bobby gave it to me. So I gave it to all my cousins."* Now right in the middle of this explosion she did a complete reversal. She said something I've never heard before. We adults couldn't think of this. Only kids could say this kind of thing and make it sound right. Right in the middle of all the negativity she said, *"Santa Claus, I love, love, love you, double times half a second."* I don't even know how good that is, but it sounded pretty good to me! So I put a lot of love in my answer, you can be sure.

When Mary Beth became an adult and moved to suburban Philadelphia, she became the mother of two little ones. She wrote to me and said:

> *"Dear Santa Claus,*
> *When I was a little girl living in Pittsburgh I used to write to you. I kept every one of those letters you sent to me. I just loved them. Santa Claus, I'd like my girls to get letters from you. You know, I don't even know if you're still doing this. I don't even know if you still live in Hanover. Quite frankly, I don't even know if you're still living! If you aren't, don't bother to answer this."*

As you can see, Mary Beth hasn't changed!

Billy from Appopca, Florida, also had some negative thoughts to tell Santa one Christmas. However, he had a different way of expressing himself. He wrote every year on little sheets of paper about 4 inches high by 4 inches wide. "Don't they have bigger sheets than that in Florida," I wondered. Surely there must be a Staples or an

Office Max in Florida somewhere.

He always wrote from the bottom left-hand corner to the top right-hand corner of the page. He could write only two sentences before his paper was filled. He had to use about six of these sheets each time he wrote a letter to Santa.

Well, Billy and his mother must have had some kind of a disagreement before he sat down to write his letter one year because he wrote the following P. S. on the back of his letter.

> *"Dear Santa, instead of a baby brother I'd rather have a baby bird. Will you talk to my mommy about this?"*

Obviously he wasn't that excited about the upcoming blessed event.

In Their Own Words

Not all children are capable, as Billy was, of writing their own letters. As you might suspect, many need their parents' help because of their young ages. After all, the ideal believing time is from age three through age six. That's why, when I deliver my "Letters to Santa" talk during the Christmas holiday season, I ask parents in the audience to let the child's voice come through when they are writing letters to Santa for their youngsters. "If you are going to sit down with your child and write a letter, let it be the child's words—not yours," I tell them. "If you want to write a letter, write your own letter! Write your own age down, too, and then I will know how to answer it. However, if you are writing for a child, write what the child is saying because the child is going to be funnier than you could ever hope to be."

Not long after I gave one of those talks at Millersville University, I received a letter from Linda, and I know I got through to at least one mother because at the bottom of the letter it said, "As dictated by Linda, age 4." I could tell Mother was writing for Linda because of the words that could only come from a child. You need to know this as background—that Linda was a very religious little gal. She talked about God and she talked about Jesus. There was no doubt in her mind about the difference between Jesus and Santa Claus.

Well, right in the middle of her letter she wrote,

> *"God is great and he loves grapes."*

Now, I said to myself, "Okay, so do I." However, that sentence puzzled me, and I have to get the bottom of everything when I don't understand it. That's the way I am.

If I know where the letter comes from, it is not unusual for me to place a telephone call when I have a question. So I called Linda's mother and told her, "It says here that God is great and he loves grapes." I asked if she could tell me what the connection was. Linda's mother replied, "I haven't the slightest idea. Do you remember you told us just to write it down? And you said we don't have to understand it."

I said, "Well, she had to have a reason for saying that. I know how she feels about God. You tell me, does Linda like grapes?"

"Oh," she said, "She loves them! As a matter of fact, that is her favorite snack food."

I then inquired, "Do you know if she was eating grapes when she dictated this letter to you?" She thought for a few seconds and then answered, "As a matter of fact, she was." At that moment, I quickly replied, "Okay, that explains it!" I had my answer! Linda loves God—Linda loves grapes—God loves grapes.

One mother who clearly never heard my talk was from Baldwin, New York. In the letter she wrote for her son Mario, she obviously wanted to make a very strong point because the letter was written as if to say, "I am boss in this family, Santa Claus. And I want you to know it."
Right in the middle of the letter, she wrote,

> *"Mario tries to be a good boy. He would like to have a farm tractor, which you are all out of."*

I'm sure she was thinking, "Maybe you think you're Santa Claus, but you better not have any farm tractors! At least not for our house!"

Hide and Seek

Kaia, from Chippewa Falls, Wisconsin wrote to me for years and years, until she was well into her teens. When she wrote her first letter, she was four years old. In her letter she said,

> *"I'm going to have some candy for you and I'm going to hide it under the couch."*

I thought it was thoughtful of her to tell me where to find the candy. I probably wouldn't have thought of looking under the couch.

In her next letter, it was obvious that Kaia was growing up. She had begun sending illustrations along with her letters. She wanted to prove to Santa Claus that she had

Dear Santa, A lot has happened since last Christmas. I have an older brother, Rob, a sister, Shelley, and I have a new baby sister, Sara, at my Dads. I'm in first grade now, and I'm a brownie. I've been trying to be a good girl and help my Mommy. I would like two things for Christmas—a baby bright doll and a premie cabbage patch girl. Can you find me in Florida at Grandpa Smiths house? Did you get the cheese I sent you? I hope you liked it. I Love you. From Kaia. 6

some talent. She sent a beautiful drawing. However, she also had a concern. She asked,

"Do you think you will be able to find me in Florida at Grandpa Smiths house?"

Why wouldn't I be able to find her at Grandpa Smith's house in Florida? Can there be more than one Grandpa Smith in Florida? The letter went on to say,

"Did you get the cheese I sent you?"

I knew that Kaia would not bring this subject up unless—what? There was cheese on the way!

A few days later I went into the post office to pick up my mail. In my post office box I found a card that read, "Article too large for the box," and I took it to the front window.

The window clerk was new and did not know me—and I certainly did not know him. After I gave him the card, he went into the back and soon returned carrying a "wheel" of cheese. Boy, are they huge!

He lifted it up and placed it on the counter. Then he looked at me and said, "Well, there must be some mistake here." I asked, "What is the mistake?" He said, "This is addressed to Santa Claus." So I again asked, "Well, what is the mistake?" He replied, "Well, I can't give you this cheese just because you say you're Santa Claus." Rather indignantly I said, "I am Santa Claus, and that cheese belongs to me."

The postmaster, whom I had known for many years, overheard and walked up behind the clerk. He winked at me and said, "Is there a problem here?"

The clerk replied, "Yes, I think there is. This fellow says he is Santa Claus and he wants this cheese."

"He is Santa Claus. Give him the cheese," said the postmaster.

The clerk slid the cheese over to me and looked around sheepishly. He leaned over and said, "Well, I didn't know you were Santa Claus."

I told him I was expecting cookies from Laurie in Richmond. "I don't want to have to go through this every time I get something too large for the box," I said. "No," he said emphatically, "You won't have to go through this again, because now I know who you are!"

We talked a bit longer and by the end of our conversation we both had some laughs.

As for Kaia, she continued to write to me for years, and she always sent me a picture with every letter.

Like Kaia, a little girl named Desirée from Quarryville, Pennsylvania, had a concern of her own, which she revealed in the following letter.

"I'm sorry about anything I've done bad. Please forgive me. I hope you will bring me a horse. I know we are middle class, but I still want a horse."

Who in the world told this young lady that she was middle class? She was seven years old. Isn't that a little early for a child to be told she is middle class?

Then Desirée wrote,

> *"P.S. Please bring me 13 toys."*

Not 12, not 14, but 13.

Short and Sweet

Some of the funniest letters are the shortest ones—like these letters from Michael and Dvora. Michael wrote,

> *"There are a lot of things I don't want so I won't write them down."*

I kind of like those types of letters.

Dvora wrote,

> *"I don't have such a long list this year, because I thought if I didn't have such a long list, then maybe you'd get me more of what I want and less of what I don't want."*

However, a young boy named Scott wrote the shortest letter I ever received. He wrote,

> *"Dear Santa, I don't want no soap. Love, Scott."*

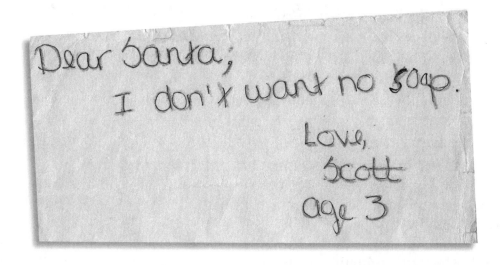

I guess you know what Scott had in mind. If he didn't get "no soap," he would not have to take "no baths." Of course, my compassion went out to his parents. I wrote back and said, "Oh, yes, you're getting soap, Scott. Everybody gets soap. Even Rudolph gets soap." So I figured I made some points with Scott's parents. I'm sure they were saying, "Right on, Santa."

As a tribute to Scott, I invite you to read my first children's book with the title, *I Don't Want No Soap.* I believe you will enjoy the rest of my answer to him. I often wonder where Scott is today. Perhaps he is in college studying English grammar.

Spelling Doesn't Count

When you read the following letters, you might want to excuse the children's spelling and punctuation. These errors are part of the charm of the letters from my little friends and they give me an extra chuckle when I read them.

The first letter is from Donna, a young girl who said she enjoyed school. She wrote a long letter, and I would like you to read some of it. Keep in mind that Donna was six years old and in first grade when she wrote her letter.

> *"When I grow up, I want to be a teacher. I like to help my mommie cook. So I want to teach kids something like Home Ecomonis."*

That's pretty close, isn't it?

> *"But, I won't yell at them if they are bad. I used to have a dog named Arlo. He had a 'hard attach.' My mommie said, Do you think him and Rudolph would of becam freinds? I have lots of freinds. My boyfriend's name is Charlie. He's pretty fat. They call him Charlie the Tuna."*

Now, remember folks, Donna is in first grade and already has a boyfriend.

> *"My mommie wants to bake you some cookies. Do you like oatmeal proon cookies? There my favrite kind."*

Now if oatmeal prune cookies are her favorite kind, don't you see that they had to be my favorite kind, too?

Donna ended her letter with the following.

"I got to take a bath. I don't like baths. Does Rudof take baths? Give Rudolph a kiss for me. P.S. My friends call me 'Dingy' becase I'm not very smart sometimes."

I hope she doesn't take that to heart, because I thought she sounded pretty smart.

I wrote back to Donna with the following reply.

"Dear Donna,
I knew something special was in the air when two of my Brownies from the post office came running over here to my cabin and were all out of breath. They handed me your letter and said they wanted to stay around until I answered it. They wanted to give it to Zip, my special delivery reindeer, as quickly as possible so that you would get an early answer. The Brownies are so excited they can hardly stand still.

It is always good news to Mrs. Santa and me to know that you like school and want to grow up to be a teacher. I guess you know Mrs. Santa teaches kindergarten during the summer. I am sure your mommy likes it when you help with the baking and cooking. Now you tell your mommy that my favorite cookie happens to be oatmeal prune cookies, too. After all, who has to be 'on the go' more than Santa?

Maybe Mrs. Santa and your mommy could swap recipes. Mrs. Santa makes a good snowdrop sugar cookie. I am almost embarrassed to tell you that I ate six of them just while I was writing my letter to you. To top it off, Mrs. Santa brought me some hot Ovaltine and I just love that.

I am sorry your dog, Arlo, had to go to Dog Heaven, but

at least we know he will have a happy life there. I am sure he and Rudolph would have become friends. Maybe you would like to see a picture of one of Rudolph's dog friends. His name is Olra."

As you can see, that is Arlo spelled backwards.

"It was nice of your boyfriend, Charlie, to help you with your letter. I know you call him 'Charlie the Tuna,' but you tell Charlie that I am a little on the tuna side myself. I'd rather be a tuna than a minnow.

Yes, Rudolph does take baths and so should you. Well, actually, Rudolph takes showers, not baths. Because you were so kind to send Rudolph a kiss, he wanted to send you his noseprint. I hope to hear from you next year, and I'll be seeing you Christmas Eve. Bye now.
Love, Santa."

Following are letters from a school in York, Pennsylvania. I do believe the teachers at this school must have had their hands full. See if you agree.

"Dear Santa Claus,
I want it to snow evry day of the year. And you better make it. Because if you don't. I will not leive a snack for you to get fater and mabey you will lose some wait. And not be so fat. How much do you waghe Santa claus?"

"Now I all most forgot. I want a bike for Christmas a lots more you haft to find out the rest or you can read my brain.

I heard rain deer up on my rofe last year and I better hear them this year and thair better be 8 rain deer too. GOOD BUY! Your freand, Angela."

―――――――――――――――――

"Dear Saint Nicholas,
Are you really fat Santa Claus? How do your reindeer fly?

Dear Santa Claus,
I want it to snow evry day of the year. And you better make it. Becouse if you don't. I will not leive a snack for you to get fater and mabey you will lose some wait! And not be so fat, how much do you waghe Santa claus?

Bow I all most forgot I want a want a bike for Christmas a lots more you haft to find out the rest or you can read my brain.

I heard rain deer up on my rofe last year and I better hear them this year and thair better be 8 rain deer too GOOD BUY!

Your freand
Angela

How can your elves make so many toys? How can you take your toys around the world so quick? How much do you weigh?"

Now we get to the heart of the letter. I believe this little guy lives in a fantasy world.

"Here is what I want for Christmas, all the transformers, a million dollars, a mansion, a cheauffer driven limozine, 1 billion stickers, all the candy in the world, 5 warehouses, all the toy stores in the world, my own universe, and last but not least a new bike.
Your friend, John."

I think maybe Santa Claus could help out with the new bike, but the rest of the requests are 'out of this world'!

"Dear Santa Claus
Hi! How are you doing! How's Mrs. Claus doing. You know
I have been getting good grades. How are the elves doing.
And also how are the reindeer. You now I don't have enough
money to buy my mom perfume. And I don't even have enogh
money for my dad's cigars. And my sisters book. And why
I forgot what my other sister wants. But I will remember. I
really want a dollhouse.
Your friend, Carrie.
P.S. I really cannot think."

Jeremy said,

"Dear Santa,
How are you today. If your so smart then guess what I want for
Christmas santa. I will give you a hint it starts with a g and
ends with a n. can you think of it. Shucks. I thot you had it."

Dear Santa, How are today. If your so smart then guess what. I want for Christmas santa. I will give you a hint it starts with a g and ends with a n. can you think of it. shucks. I thot you had it. its a gun, zazr tag, Bmx Bike, and thats all.

Sincerely Jeremy

I guess Jeremy forgot how smart Santa is because I had that riddle figured out before I read "Shucks." He goes on to say,

"It's a gun, zazrtag, BMX Bike, and thats all."

This letter from Jaime is a little different.

"Dear Santa Claus,
My religion is Jewish. I only believe in you a little bit. The part about the presents."

Is this what you expected from these kids?

David wrote a long letter, but the thing that intrigued me the most was the P.S. It says,

"P.S. I also want five of something, but I can't remember what."

I guess Santa was supposed to remember what David wanted.

This next letter is now so faint because I've had it for such a long time. Laura wrote,

"I have been a good little girl and I haven't fought with my brothers for a whole week. For Christmas, I want a stuffed lion and a stuffed tiger. I don't know what else I want, but I want love for my grandpa and my grandma, and my other grandpa and my mom and my dad and my brothers and my great grandpa. I don't like to mention how old he is, but at least he is still living and breathing."

Way to hang in there, Grandpa!

Robert said,

"Please bring me a pair of roller blades..."

He sent along a picture of his footprint. I suppose that was so I could get the right size. There's nothing like being helpful.

I don't know if this next little guy was in trouble or not. His name is Joseph and he wrote,

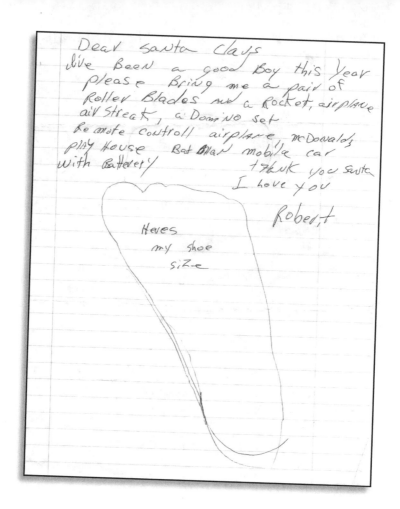

Dear Santa Claus
I've Been a good Boy this Year
please Bring me a pair of
Roller Blades and a Rocket, airplane
air streak, a Domino set
Remote controll airplane, McDonalds
play House Bat man mobile car
with Battery

thank you Santa
I love you

Robert

Heres
my shoe
size

"Dear Santa,
my mom let me find your suit in the attic. I asked if I could try to put it on and my mom said I could. Then I asked my mom what ever happened to Santa", and she answered, 'He died.' "So I don't know why I even believe in you. I must be insane. I saw all my presents. I don't even think you fly in the sky."

And the letter was signed,

"Your insane friend, Joseph."

Jeff wrote a very short letter.

"I'm a good kid, but I'm going to keep the fireplace burning all night long anyhow."

I guess he was saying, "Go ahead, Santa, if you want to take your chances. You've heard of a hot foot—you could get more than a hot foot!" Then he added a P.S. that said,

"I was just kidding about the fireplace."

I guess Jeff had second thoughts.

This one is pretty different, too.

"Dear Santa,
I want roller skates that fit me. And I hope you and Mrs.
Claus are both fine. How are the elves doing? I hope they're
doing good. I have lots of pets. Watch out for them—
especially Theodore. Have a happy Christmas, even though
I celebrate Hanukkah. I still like people who are Christian.
It isn't fair. They should have a Hanukkah Man. Love,
Debra."

Here's another one I think you will appreciate.

"I've been trying to be extremely good, and nice. Could
you say hello to Rudolph for me? I hope you can take care
of Rudolph. I'm a good writer, and I've been writing a
story about Rudulf, and I would really like to know what
Rudulf's mother's name is. Since Rudulf's father's name is
Donner, I think Rudolph's mother's name is Deener."

I guess that's a good possibility. Throughout the rest of the letter, this child asked for specific presents for other family members. Up to this point, her spelling was very good, so I'm not sure what happened here. She said,

"My mother wants the Billy Joel Inicent Man and Dad
wants reall specail collone."

Casey wrote,

"Dear Santa,
Hi! How are you? I'm fine. How's Mrs. Claus? Did you get
the reindeer all warmed up? You will get a lot of cookies
and hot chocolate. Or you can have coffee. You were so
nice last year. You gave me everything I wanted! I want

Consrux Thundering Trax, Electronic Battleship, No war, a car for everybody in the world, and Hewy Lewis to play a concert for my mom. I'll leave a little present for you under the tree.

Is that alright with you? I hope so. Your biggest friend, Casey."

I think Casey is laying it on pretty thick when he signs his letter, "Your biggest friend." I shouldn't have had any trouble getting Hewy Lewis to play a concert for his mom, should I? I notice this letter is dated 1986, so that tells you when Hewy must have been popular.

Kelly wrote,

"I'd like to have a horse/pony more than anything else in the whole world. Please don't get me anything else. Please don't get me anything for my birthday, either. The horse pony would take care of my birthday and my Christmas gifts for as long as they live."

Oh, dear. I guess when they die, I'm in trouble.

Poetic License

Some of the children like to write poetry. First, Jodi asked,

"How are your reindeer?"

Then she got right to it. She said,

*"If I were a reindeer. I might meet a snake.
I'd run in the forest and jump in the lake."*

You can't rhyme much better than snake and lake, can you? Then she said,

"How do you like my poem? I hope you do. I love you. And I hope you do, to."

I told her I did love both of us. Aren't we to love our neighbors as ourselves?

Mary, from State College, Pennsylvania, wrote poetry, too. Hers was a little more extensive and she called it

> *"Christmas."*
> *"Christmas is coming and Santa Claus too,*
> *With his bag of toys and reindeer, too.*
> *All the toys are scattered all over the place,*
> *And when Mommy sees the place, she makes a face.*
> *And when Daddy rolls out of bed and sees the place, he faints,*
> *And when Chris rolls out of bed and sees the place,*
> *He says Wow, what a place!"*

They do say repetition is effective.

Tired of Waiting

Michael was a bit testy when he wrote,

> *"I have bin waited for one year for this day and now it*
> *has come. Do you know what day that is? It's Christmas.*
> *I have waited threw JANUARY, FEBRUARY, MARCH,*
> *APRIL, MAY, JUNE, JULY, AUGUST, SEPTEMBER,*
> *OCTOBER, NOVEMBER, and now it is here and you'd*
> *better come, too."*

I think Michael just wanted Santa to know that he knew the months of the year.

Brian, I believe, must be a philosopher somewhere today. He said,

> *"Dear Santa,*
> *I'm really glad to live on the earth and if there was no*
> *Christmas, I probbley wouldn't be liveing now. That's just*
> *an opinion."*

He goes on to tell me it's Bri for short and Brains for his nickname. I especially like his P.S.

> *" P.S. I do think you're cool dood."*

It's easy to be a "cool dood" up here at the North Pole.

A True Believer

This next letter is one I just can't shortcut.

> *"Dear Santa,*
> *I guess I'll start this letter by telling you my name. It is*
> *Amy and I'm in third grade. My teacher's name is Mrs.*
> *Marshall, and she has no children. Do you have any new*
> *relitives? I do. She's now my aunt. Her name is Val. You*
> *won't like to hear this, but I'm the only one in my class*
> *that belives in you. I think I'll beleave in you until I'm 20*
> *years old. Even older than that. Well, at least one more*
> *year! But what I want to know is how do you get around*
> *the world in one night? I know your rain dear can fly, but*
> *how do you get around the world in one night? How old*
> *are you? I'm eight this year. And my birthday is September*
> *5, 1973. If you tell me your birthday I'll send you a present*
> *every year."*

Wasn't that a nice offer? Now, I don't like to say this, but this child wasn't true to her word. I wrote her and I told her my birthday is October 15. And that's the last I ever heard from her!

Amy continued,

> *"How is Mrs. Santa? And I forgot to ask you how you*
> *are. How are you? I'm fine. I never see the doll, Priscilla,*
> *anymore. Tell Rudolph we will put out some carrots for*
> *him and the other reindear will get some too. Plus we will*
> *put out some extra peanut brittle. Rudolph can have some.*
> *And for you we will put out some peanut brittle and milk*
> *and maybe even some cookies.*
>
> *This is what I want for Christmas, a pocket camra, a whatch*
> *and walet, a nightstand, dresser, desk, and thats all.*
>
> *Would you take a picture of Rudolph and the other*
> *reindear hooked up to the sleigh on Christmas night and*
> *put it on the table. And could one of the Brownies take a*

pitcure of you and your wife. And one just of you and one just of Rudolph. Suzie wants a ten speed girls bike. And Mom and Dad are hanging up there stockings on Christmas Eve. I'm writing this letter early so you can write back. Tell Rudolph my first oarl book report was about a dear. How old is Rudolph?
Is he married?"

Did you know Rudolph is married? Oh, yes, Rudolph is married. His wife's name is Pinky. She has a pink nose and Rudolph, as you know, has a red nose. They look so cute together and they get along great. They had their first little deer eighteen years ago. Pinky would like to go along on the trip with Rudolph, but Rudolph says, "It's better if you stay home and then when you have that big welcome home party for me we will be together for another whole year." They have this worked out, folks, believe me. They don't need a counselor.

Amy goes on to say,

"I can't wait until Christmas Eve. It seems theres so many dolls that theres no more to make. But I'm sure Mrs. Santa will make one more this year. Tell here I hope she will come up with one.

My mother says for her honey moon she went to the Nourth Pole and saw you, Santa. Do you remember that?"

Sure, how could I forget?

"That's where I'm going for my honey moon, and I'll meet Rudolph in person.

I like that pitcure of you on the stationery that you write on to me. Do you have littel things that you sprinkle on kids eyes so they won't wake up? Who is the oldest Brownie? Do you know that? And how old is he? Are there any girl Brownies?"

Sure, there are a lot of girl Brownies. We have equal opportunity up here.

"Am I getting coal in my stocking? Do you know how many houses are there in the whole wourld? I ask pretty hard quistcions, don't I? "

Yeah, I'd say she does! And then Amy shows me some of her artwork, which I thought you might like to see.

(Amy's artwork)

To Do List

Do some of you recall what we used to call little work charts? Maybe you know them as chore charts. They're kind of like a graph, where you list the days of the week and what you want the child to do on the different days. I don't see a lot of those around anymore, but I'm sure they exist.

I thought this was pretty cute. One child sent me a copy of her chart.

"Pick up toys."

It looks like she picked up her toys every day but Tuesday. That's not bad.

"Help with the barn chores without being scolded."

Every day! Good for her.

"Feed the dogs without goofing off."

This was interesting. The dogs only got fed on Wednesdays and Thursdays, according to the chart. I wouldn't stop for a visit on Monday or Tuesday because the dogs could be in a bad mood by then!

"Don't sass mommie."

Every other day.

"Stop twisting hair."

Oh dear, no stars for that one.

"Get dressed in the morning."

Now this chore is really amusing to me. According to the chart, this child only got dressed on Tuesdays and Thursdays.

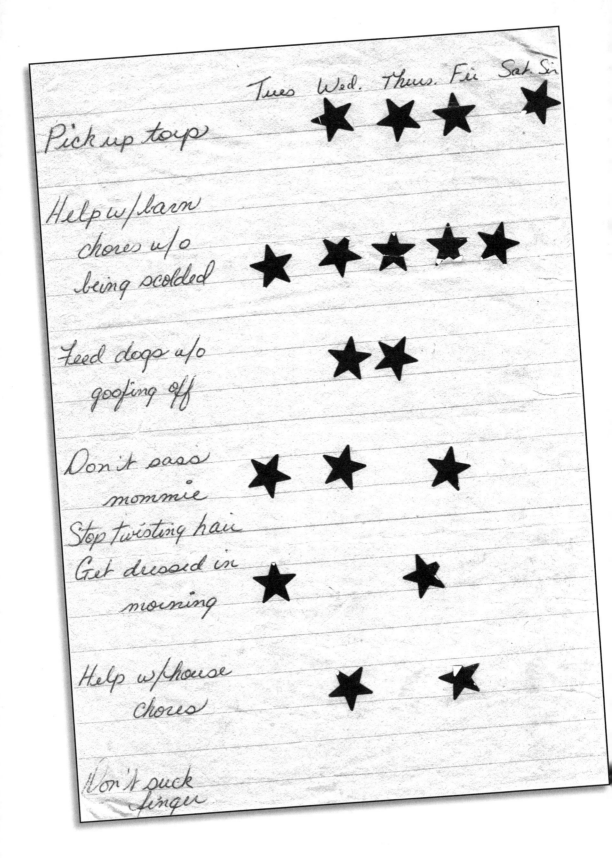

	Tues	Wed.	Thurs.	Fri	Sat	Si
Pick up toys		★	★	★		★
Help w/farm chores w/o being scolded	★	★	★	★	★	
Feed dogs w/o goofing off		★	★			
Don't sass mommie		★	★		★	
Stop twisting hair						
Get dressed in morning		★		★		
Help w/house chores			★		★	
Don't suck finger						

One Last Letter and a Change of Heart

Kathy Jo from Elizabethtown, Pennsylvania, typed her letter. She said,

"This is the last year I'm writing to you. I'm 11 years old and I'm 5'3." I have blonde hair and I wear glasses. My Christmas list is as follows: A blouse, Sears Christmas catalog, page 93, number 1, $20.00, size small."

And then she went on to list everything and every page number and the name of the store. Then she said,

"I have a dog named Snoopy. She barks at strangers. She is a beagle. It's probably cold up North. It's very cold here in Pennsylvania. Since this is the last letter I'm writing to you, I wish your family and your elves a Merry Christmas every year."

When children are at the point where they are not sure about Santa Claus or no longer believe in Santa Claus, I will say something like this to them.

"I know you have heard that some of the children don't believe in Santa Claus anymore. Well, let me tell you that you can always believe in me, and I will always believe in you. You will find, as you grow up, that Santa is not just a man in a red suit—he is the Spirit of Giving and Love. There is no age limit to that."

Another letter from Elizabethtown, Pennsylvania, was written by Robert. He said,

"I know one thing I want for Christmas, and that is to be happy for what I get."

Just as I was thinking how nice it is to get letters like that once in awhile, Robert expressed a quick change of heart.

"If I get three things that will be okay with me," he wrote. "If I get two things, that's still okay with me. But if I only get one thing, that's not okay!"

A Private Matter

Mrs. Santa came to the rescue in this next letter. Included in Rachel's letter to me was a little pink envelope addressed to Mrs. Claus. As you will see, this was very personal and this was not a question for Santa. Rachel wrote,

> *"Dear Mrs. Clause,*
> *Could you please give me a bra with holders. I think it is*
> *size 32A. Thanks. Love, Rachel."*

When writing back to Rachel, I had Mrs. Santa type a little note to her so she knew this was kept very private.

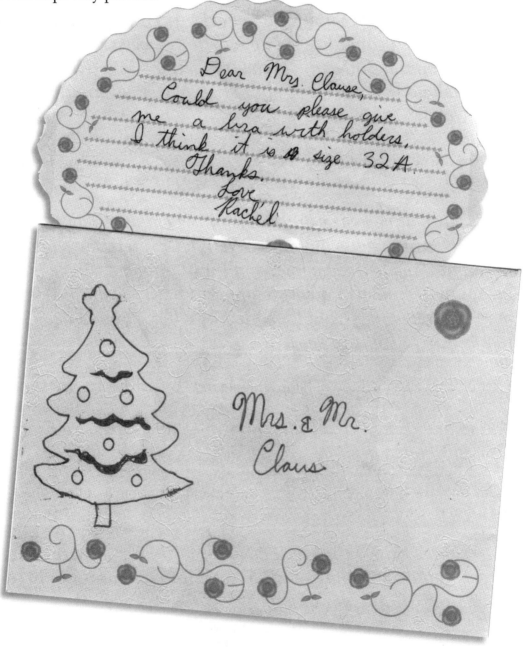

Tell Me the Truth

Molly wrote to me twice. Her first letter was a sweetheart. I often wished I could have met Molly in person. I want you to pay particular attention to the spelling.

"Dear Santa,
I am Molly. How are you doing? I am fine. I just have insteructions for you. When I write something in ink it means I really want it. When I write something in pencil I want it but not as much as something in ink. When I write something in ink & pencil I want it a lot & kind of don't care."

Well, I didn't want Molly to have any concerns, so I reassured her by answering,

"I will follow your instructions about what you wrote in pencil and in ink. I understand it perfectly."

When Molly wrote her second letter, she was rather specific in that one. It seemed that Molly really was growing up quickly. She wrote,

"Dear Santa Claus,
Have I been a good girl this year? You don't have to say yes because you think you'll hurt my fellings just let it out!
I ❤ U
Molly"

She simply was trying to do the very best she could to be good. If she did something bad, she wanted to know what it was. Here again, I wanted to reassure Molly so I replied,

"Don't you worry—if I have something to tell you, I will not hold back. As you say, 'Let it out.'"

As it turns out, I have never met her, but I did discover she is the daughter of one of the dentists in the practice I visit twice a year in York, Pennsylvania.

Robert asked an unusual question.

"Santa, why are girls such fruits? Do you think girls are fruits?"

26

Of course I had to stick up for the girls, right? I certainly could not agree with him on this one. I think Robert's mind was on fruit because he then added this.

"P.S. Mommy is gonna leave some fruit out for you. Does reindears like fruit?"

Christopher wrote seeking help with a problem and the truth about Santa Claus. First, he wrote,

"Dear Santa,
I am having a hard time with these girls in school. Could you think of a way to stop this? Would you please put a sign that you are true like a peace of your shirt or your belt. Some people at school say you are not true but I believe in you. The reason I ask to leave a sign of you is to prove that you are true to my class."

Notice the spelling of peace? Well, I don't try to encourage kids to hang on if they are questioning the truth about Santa Claus; however, in this case I happened to have an excellent "piece" of me to send him. One of my previous letters included a gift that was knitted especially for Santa Claus—a nosewarmer! Who better to make good use of a nosewarmer than Santa?

I responded to Christopher with the following reply.

"Well, Chris, since you asked for something that would prove that I am true, I am sending you one of my nosewarmers. You must know how cold it gets on the big trip, and my nosewarmers help keep my nose warm and also keep it from getting red. Mrs. Santa makes sure I am bundled from head to toe and she always makes sure I don't leave without my nosewarmer. She has knitted me a bunch of them, so she won't mind if I send you this one."

I think Christopher had a soft spot for Mrs. Santa, too, because he ended his letter by saying,

"I love you very much and your wife to. Say hello to your wife for me."

Adam, age 7, was also questioning the truth about Santa Claus. Apparently his friend, Kenny, had a very strong influence on him.

"Dear Santa,
My friend Kenny doesn't believe in you. I hope you have a Happy Christmas. Santa, I believe in you because I like you very, very much, but when Kenny is around I just say do you like Santa and he just won't let me say I believe in you. But, I still do, just not when Kenny's around because he doesn't believe in you."

A boy named Ben wanted to make sure Santa knew exactly what he wanted for Christmas and had a plan to make sure there were no mistakes. At the bottom of his letter was a complete collage of color photographs of each item. He even listed the name of the website for his Dragonball z guys!

He also wasn't sure whether to believe in Santa. Although Ben was 14-years-old when he wrote this letter, I thought his logic was very good when he said,

"Kids at school say you don't exist but then how am I getting letters and presents from you once a year?"

His final words on the subject were,

"The whole issue makes my head hurt!"

Keeping Ben's age and concerns in mind, I wrote the following reply.

"Hi Ben,
I know you are almost fourteen and I am glad you still believe in me, because I certainly believe in you. Mrs. Santa believes in me and she is a lot older than fourteen! If I

don't exist, I don't know who is writing this letter, do you? I don't want this issue to make your head hurt. Just clear your head and accept the fact that you just got a letter from me.

I can see you are really into the dragonball z guys, so I will try to add to your collection. When I told Mrs. Santa about this, she didn't even know there were z guys. She knew there were "r" guys and she knew there were "y's" guys, so even she can learn something at her age. By the way, those were neat pictures you drew on the back of your letter."

Truthfully, I wasn't too sure about the picture of me. His Santa Claus picture looked a little mean and it said, "Chick Magnets" on the front of my shirt. I don't think Mrs. Santa would like it if I wore a shirt that said that!

"Don't I always wrap your gifts every year? Actually, I don't wrap them myself, but I do have some Brownie wrappers who do this. They listen to rap music when they do their wrapping, so I have to leave the room because I can't stand rap music. If you want to do me a little favor this year, leave me a snack of Utz's potato chips and Snyder's pretzels. I will bring them back for Mrs. Santa because she just loves those two things. Every time I come to Hanover, it seems like it is getting bigger, especially on the south and north ends of the town. There are so many new stores in the strip back of North Hanover Mall. I am sure you have been in almost every one of them.

Mrs. Santa just stopped by to tell me she is having some trouble with the zipper machine over in the doll workshop. As soon as I finish your letter, I will have to go over there and get things straightened out. Last year it was the button-holer machine that went on the blink. Now this year it seems like the zipper machine isn't working right.

Well, Ben, get things ready for me at your house on Christmas Eve. I will be anxious to come to your place. Love, Santa."

They Said It

Lisa's letter was brief and to the point.

"Dear Santa,
I want a art easel for Christmas. If you don't want to get
me a easel you don't have to get me anything. Love, Lisa."

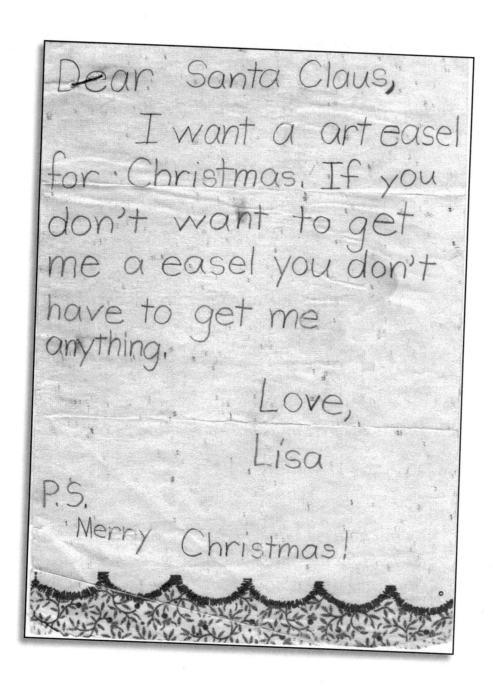

Oh, the little ones know about money, too. Just listen to this next letter from Chris.

"Dear Santa,
I have been good this year. I have a long list of things
I want. If you can't bring all the toys I want just bring
money. How is your wife? How are you? How are your
reindeer? From, Chris."

Heather needs someone to understand the struggles her family has gone through just to put up their Christmas tree. She wrote as part of her letter,

"We are having problomes with our Christmas tree at hom.
It will not fit in our stand. The stump is to fat for it. But
we got it up."

If at first you don't succeed, keep trying!

I think this little one learned sarcasm a little early, don't you?

"Dear Santa,
My name is Sean and I am 3 years old. According to my
sister, Erynn, I have been good most of the time this year.
But what does she know? Probably nothing!"

One little girl's ending paragraph made me a little sad. She wrote,

"I want Christmas to come up soon. I want it to be over with."

Oh, what a great attitude this little gal had.

"Dear Santa,
Deep down in my heart, I would truly want a taperecorder
& two Cb raidios for chrismas, but if I don't get them I just
won't be lucky. Sinsearly yous from Dana. I love you lots.
XOXO."

There is no bitterness there.

My friend, Randy, says,

"Don't let me down. If you don't come this year, I will look for you next year."

Here again, there is no animosity, and Randy wasn't going to give up on Santa Claus. I believe he is one of those positive thinkers.

It sounds to me like Jim was trying to build Santa Claus up to the point where Santa couldn't refuse to bring him what he wanted when he says,

"You are so nice. You are so perrffecket. You are great."

In case that didn't work, he added,

"You will find some cookies and milk on the right side of the tree."

It almost sounds like a bribe, doesn't it?

I guess it is natural for my little friends to be concerned about my health and Stacey expressed her concern in her letter. You will want to pay close attention to the spelling.

"Dear Santa,
I want a bunch of things for Christmas. But I don't want
to be mean so I cut it down to 3. I want a t.v., Winnie the
Pooh and Fozz ball for the whole family. Christmas is
speacail to me because your coming to my house. I got
something speacail for you. I hope your not lack toss and
tolerit. Then you can't have what I'm giving you. I love
you Santa. Your friend, Stacey."

How thoughtful of Stacey to watch out for me. Well, I can tell you that Santa is not lactose intolerant and he loves to drink chocolate milk!

A child wrote from Spring Grove, Pennsylvania, with some good news for Santa!

"Dear Santa and Mrs. Clause,
Hello! How are you doing? Tell Rudolph they are going to
decrease the stinky smell of Spring Grove."

This reference to the stinky smell of Spring Grove goes back one year to my mention of the unpleasant odor created by a chemical used in manufacturing paper at the paper mill. Every paper mill deals with this situation. I told this child that Rudolph always told me he thought it smelled like sauerkraut when we approached the town.

I did remind him that the paper plant provided a lot of jobs to a lot of people, but I guess this little boy was concerned I might not come to his house if the smell in the town was too bad. I did reassure him by letting him know it would not be a problem.

Quite a List

I don't get too many letters written in cursive, so I knew this next letter writer was a bit older. She began her letter with the following list.

Christmas List
underwear
socks
turtle necks
sweaters
jeans
pants
cardigens
hooded sweatshirts
twill shirts
Denim shirts
wind suits
speedometer for bike
light for bike
turning signals for bike
jean shorts
three in one jacket
overalls
shoes (size 7)
T-shirts
outfits
shirt and pants
1 piece P.J.'s
belt

longsleeve shirts
Leather granny
boots
Sebago (brown
shoes)
sweater
granny boots
two piece polar
fleece
video painter
Geosafari
computer game with
school subjects, and
puzzles
Monopoly gameboy
game
basketball
ball that is soft
bike
skates
merlin magic set
snowboots
doodads for my
stockings

As you can see, she had a list of 38 items. I suppose she may have realized this list was a bit much because her parting paragraph said,

> *"I don't expect you to bring me all of this stuff. It's just an idea list!"*

Either she was very optimistic or had the desire to see just how many things she could get out of her long list. In any event, when I answered her letter, I let her know I would bring her as much as I could get in one of my large stretch bags.

The final sentences of a letter written by a girl named Brandy were interesting. She wrote,

> *"You are my best friend if you will get me a ten speed."*

It looked like our friendship had some stipulations. Then she went on to say,

> *"It dos not matter."*

Well, I'm sure it did matter, but I'm not sure why she said it didn't. Either way, I hope she was happy.

Adriane wrote a full-page letter, but there were a few sentences that stood out for me. She started her letter like this.

> *"I hate people who do not belive in you."*

I'd like to think that was just an emotional statement, and she was simply making her point in a very strong manner.

I was quite surprised at the last couple of lines when she said,

> *"I will have a surprise for you. You got it for me."*

I'm not sure that's what she meant, but that is exactly what she said. And then on the back of her letter she had this very nice drawing. I'm surprised whenever I see a skinny Santa Claus!

Another method of getting the message across to Santa is shown in the next letter, which has a complete grid of all pertinent gift information. Does this leave any room for doubt, Santa?

I particularly liked the box that stated simply, "You should know" in the "What is it" column. Apparently this child recognized that Santa is "in the know!"

Name	What is it?	Price	Store	Where
The Sims	A computer game where you design a house and family	$20.00	Staples or Circuit City	Tree
Lava Lamp	I hope you know	$50.00	Kohl's	Tree
Dive Mirra freestyling biking	A video game where you are riding a bike.	$40.00	KB Toys	Tree
Now 5	A CD including 3 doors down Bon Jovi and 9 days, etc.	$20.00	The Wall/ Record Town	Tree
Bop it extreme	A mind game where you quickly follow a voices command.	$15.00	Target	Tree
Topps or upper deck baseball cards	You should know.	.75	Kmart	Stocking
Gooze, any kind; green preferred	A sticky substance you can stretch, pop, mold and bounce	$5.00	KB Toys	Stocking
	Total:	$155.75		

A Laughing Matter

No matter how "in the know" Santa may be, there is a lot to be learned from children. Statistics tell us children laugh between 140 and 160 times a day. Adults laugh only 15 times a day. I hope we have raised that adult average with the stories and letters you have just read.

Mrs. Santa often says, "You know, sometimes I think you really are just four years old." I never apologize for that. It is fun being four….or five….or six….or whatever age I have to be when I write my letters. It stretches my mind in the right direction—positively and with great passion.

Take this letter, for example, which I wrote in response to one I received from a little girl named Kendall from Jersey Shore, Pennsylvania. My answers are predicated on what she said to me in her letter.

"Dear Kendall,
Well, well, it still looks like you like that Barbie doll. I was just thinking how close your name comes to sounding like Barbie's boyfriend—Ken Doll. Did you ever think of that? He's pretty lucky to have a popular gal like Barbie.

I don't think they will ever get married, though. Barbie's too much of a career doll. And Ken has trouble keeping a job, too. I don't know what his problem is, but I suspect he might be a little lazy. Sometimes he doesn't even shave and that really upsets Barbie. She calls him 'Stubbles.'"

For you parents who don't know anything about Ken dolls and Barbie dolls, there is one Ken doll that is not clean shaven. So I know whereof I speak.

"Kendall, I think Mrs. Santa must be working on a special surprise for you this year. Every time she goes past me and sees that I am writing to you, she nudges me and winks. If she didn't have a sleeveless dress on, I would think she might have something up her sleeve! She's been wearing some of those designer jeans recently since she lost some

weight. Yesterday she had some bellbottoms on. She said they are coming back again. I didn't know they went anywhere.

Rudolph is as happy as I have ever seen him. He and his wife, Pinky, just came back from Merry Mountain. He said they went up there for a retreat. My one ear doesn't work too well and I thought he said they went up there to eat. He explained it to me later in my good ear.

Oh, I can hear my Brownie Choir practicing now. They have a big program tomorrow night. Mrs. Santa has a solo and she is going to be singing a song called, 'I Walk Alone.' I don't know why she picked that number because I'm usually with her everywhere she goes. Next week it is my turn and I'm going to sing, 'When the Rolls Are Called up Yonder, I'll Be There for Dinner.'

Oh my! Rudolph just called to tell me one of his reindeer has the hiccups, so he wants me to come over to the reindeer ranch and scare him so the hiccups will go away. I have so many different jobs. I'll be seeing you Christmas Eve, Kendall, so go to bed early. Bye now.
Love, Santa."

We all need to find something every day to make us laugh. If you learn to laugh at yourself, you will always have something to laugh at!

Chapter Two
Oldsters Can be Youngsters, Too

It is amazing how many ties and friendships I have developed because of my children's ministry. There seems to be a certain sense of loyalty and "belief" among the older generations. Now in my third generation of answering these letters, I am hearing from the grandmothers who wrote to me as children and are now helping their grandchildren write to Santa.

One of the most amazing stories of longevity is of a family now living in Idylwild, California, Jack and Janet Kunkle. We first met about 44 years ago when I gave a talk in western Pennsylvania, and the Kunkles have been writing ever since that time on behalf of their children and grandchildren. Although their children are now dispersed over a few western states, they continue to write to me as well. I always hear from them at Christmastime, as well as several other times during the year.

Through the years, Mrs. Kunkle was always kind enough to keep me abreast of all the family activities. She would write four or five sheets of paper on both sides. I just loved her letters. I knew everything that was going on in the Kunkle family. I knew who was going to school and what years they were in and all of their activities. I really believe I knew more about the Kunkle children and their family than I did about my next-door neighbor, and I say that in an affectionate way.

The Kunkles even tried to visit me one Sunday many years ago, when I was living in Hanover, Pennsylvania. They had been vacationing in Gettysburg and had decided to drive to Hanover in search of Santa Claus, even though they did not know my street address. Ironically, my family and I were revisiting the battlefield in Gettysburg at the time. When we returned home, I found an envelope containing a lengthy letter from Mrs. Kunkle in my front door.

Her letter described how they followed a map from Gettysburg to Hanover and then began asking for directions to my house once they passed the Utz Potato Chip Plant. When Janet saw a man walking along the sidewalk, she told Jack to pull over and she asked the man, "Do you know where Santa Claus lives?" The man gave her a puzzled look and then responded, "North Pole, I think, Lady!" Mrs. Kunkle said, "Well, you don't even know what I'm talking about." The stranger replied, "You're right, Lady!"

Janet looked at her husband and said rather forcefully, "Keep going, Jack." Nothing was going to stop Mrs. Kunkle from finding Santa Claus. Finally, she had gotten directions to the house from a woman she stopped on the street in Hanover.

Another family with whom I have kept in touch is the Muse family from Glen Allen, Virginia. I met Larry and Mary Ann Muse through the Virginia Jaycees, and I have corresponded with them for more than 50 years. Their children used to write to me, and they liked to send Santa Claus tins of cookies.

Two more of my "old friends," Janet and her daughter, Phyllis, have been among my most loyal friends for many years. They have attended my "Letters to Santa" talk for at least 14 years. They always come early so they can get a seat in the first row. Phyllis is hearing-impaired and must read lips.

They tell me they enjoy hearing the same letters as well as the new ones I add each year. Year after year, as I watch them laughing in the front row as if they were hearing the letters for the very first time, I know they are very loyal friends.

I continue to correspond with many other wonderful people who I am also proud to call loyal friends, even though there are some I have never met in person. These long-lasting relationships are some of the best rewards of this avocation. Often, they have resulted in letters from parents and older children expressing heartfelt appreciation for our correspondence or displaying a witty sense of humor.

These handwritten letters from adults mean a great deal to me because they show me my peers understand how important this entire "children's ministry" has been to me. To know they share some of my feelings about these children is extremely gratifying.

Here are some beautiful examples of those heartfelt letters:

"Dear Santa,
Mommy is writing this letter for us as she's done in the past. This, sadly, will probably be our last letter to you. We don't want to take your valuable time. For many years you have brought smiles of joy to our faces when we received your beautifully written letters. It was very plain that you cared about each and every one of us who took the time to write to you. We were all individuals and you treated us all just that way—no form letters—but a well-thought out letter based on our own. We know that you couldn't see the children's faces when they received your letters, but take it from us—it was worth all your effort.

My brother, Gregg, is 8 now and I'm nearly 11, and we

finally admit that there is no Santa (or is there?) The only thing we want this year is to say, 'Thank You, Santa Claus' for all the beautiful memories you gave us and thousands of other children. Maybe there is no Santa, but you are about as close to it as anyone has ever come. And so, we wish you and your family a joyous, warm Christmas 1973, and thank you again for all you have given us. We love you, Mr. Gouker! Here's hoping that 1974 brings better days to this beautiful world.
Merry Christmas,
Diane and Gregg (and their Mom and Dad)."

When Diane says, "I wish you could see the smiles on the children's faces, but I know you couldn't," well, I think I can see the smiles on their faces. I believe that is one of the things that has kept me going over the last 58 years. I don't have to know these little ones individually to know my letters make them happy. I don't have to be there to see the smiles on their faces. I just know they are there. They deserve these years of fantasy and belief.

This next letter came to me in 1969.

"Dear Santa,
As I was reading your letter to my daughter, I cannot find the words to say of the look of joy, happiness and amazement that showed on her face. It brought tears to my own eyes, knowing that there is someone who cares enough to do what you are doing. To think there is someone who cares enough to take time out of his busy life to bring this happiness to children. Again I say that words cannot express my feelings for this. I only wish there were some way to show my appreciation other than this note. As far as I am concerned, there is a Santa, and that is you, whoever you are. May God bless you always for what you are doing. You asked Stephanie for her picture and this is the one she chose so that you could also see Daisy, her cat. She can't wait to see what 'Kitten Kurls' are that you are bringing for Daisy. Thanking you again."

A young man named John wrote to me for many years from Winston-Salem, North Carolina. When he was 12, he wrote a letter saying,

"Dear Santa,
I've wondered about you for some time. Now, I really found
out. You know what? It's a little bit sad, but I'm going to
have fun putting things under the tree for my little brother,
Chris. And I want to thank you for writing all those letters to
me all those years. God bless you. John."

After that, I sat down and wrote the shortest letter I have ever written:

"Dear John, you say you found out about me. I've known
about you for years. You keep writing to me and I'll keep
writing to you."

John is now the father of three children who have all written to me. He and his family lived in Naperville, Illinois, when he was a salesman for Häagen-Dazs, and John wrote to me and said, "I know you don't want money for this, Santa Claus, but maybe you can make use of these." He sent me 10 coupons for Häagen-Dazs ice cream. Later, John moved to New Jersey and was a sales representative for the Dove Company. You can guess what I received from John then.

The Snyders have been writing for three generations.

"Dear Santa,
It seems to be that time of year again. I'm writing this
letter with mixed emotions. You see, Santa, I'm a MOM.
My youngest child, Nicole, has informed me she no longer
believes in you. I don't understand her. I realize she's 10
years old and my son, Ronnie, is 17. But you see, Santa,
Christmas is for believers and dreamers. I believe! And
you are the person who has helped make past Christmas
memories something I will cherish the rest of my life.

It all started when my parents were involved with the
Red Lion Jaycees. Believe it or not, I still have my letters
you sent me 'way back then.' Both of my kids kept all of

their letters. It has become a tradition displaying the 'letter from Santa' on our refrigerator. Although this will probably be my last letter, I will certainly pass these delightful memories on to my grandchildren someday. Maybe you will still be kind enough to answer their letters.

Surely you've heard all of this before, but here it goes again. Words will never say how much I've appreciated your kindness and thoughtfulness in displaying your love for children in this manner. You see, Santa, I'm a T.E.L.L.S. aide in the Red Lion School District. I work with young children each day. I know the joy you must feel.

Please remember! Santa and Grover Gouker will be in our memories forever. THANKS FOR THE MEMORIES!"

Here is the letter from a grateful Mary Ellen, who was the beginning of three generations of another family writing to Santa Claus.

"Dear Santa Claus,
I have never believed in Santa Claus until tonight. I have just returned home from our Hershey Federation Woman's Club and I still feel the 'glow' of having had the real Santa Claus at our meeting. Your story about 'Letters to Santa Claus' touched every woman in the room. I have never seen so many tears in the members' eyes as I did when you told the story about the child who had polio. On the other hand, what a laugh we got from the letter with the long list of things wanted by the writer.

Just knowing how happy you have made 100,000 children with your letters must be very rewarding. If only we had more people to give of themselves as you are doing. May God continue to bless you!"

The following letter is from a true believer.

"Dear Mr. Gouker,
As you can see from the way I addressed this letter, 'I believe in you.' I'm sure that sentence holds much more

meaning for me now than it did four days ago. This letter has a two-fold purpose. First, as secretary of the Hummelstown P.T.A., it is my responsibility to thank you for a most enjoyable evening on Monday. I sincerely think everyone at the meeting that night was genuinely moved by your talk and, on behalf of the P.T.A., I say thank you.

Now, however, I would like to tell you how I personally felt after hearing you talk. I believe in you not as Santa Claus, or as the most important man in all the world from now until December 25th, but as a man named Grover Gouker. It is so rare to meet a fellow human being who cares as deeply and strongly as the one I met on Monday night. I could not help but feel the happiness that you expressed in speaking of all your children nor could I not feel the sorrow and compassion that you have for so many of them. But most of all, it is the love you seem to have so much of. It must give you such a sense of fulfillment to enjoy giving so much love and happiness to so many, and I'm sure you must reap tremendous rewards in the form of pleasure and happiness because you know love from the standpoint of both giving it and receiving it. I do believe in you, Mr. Gouker, as Santa Claus and as a wonderful man. God bless you."

Not all of the letters I receive from adults are sentimental. Following are some of the more humorous examples. The first one is a fun-filled letter from my friend, Sherry.

"Dear Santa,
We have been friends for a long time, and friends should always be truthful to each other. I hope that you will not be offended by my letter. If you stop by my house Christmas Eve, please leave your reindeer outside, unless they are housebroken. My mother is still trying to get the brown stains off our carpet they left last year. We don't mind if you have a snack, but Santa, last year you ate the whole thing! I'm not trying to say you are fat, but let's face it, you are a little chubby. Please be careful where you sit. I don't mind one broken chair, but two or three?

Since you fell through the roof last year, why not be like everyone else and use the door? I'll hide the key under the welcome mat.

I know you drank a shot of Southern Comfort to warm you up, but maybe you had better bring your own bottle this year. My mother was a little upset when she discovered you emptied two bottles. Is that why you have a red nose?

Santa, I really do appreciate your gifts, but what am I to do with a 10-foot corduroy boat, an electric beach ball, and two cases of Fletcher's Castoria?

Well, this is the end of my letter. I hope that we will still be good friends. Dress warm, bring your own bottle, and have a safe trip. If you know what I mean! Please give my regards to Mrs. Claus! All my love, Sherry."

Every letter deserves an answer commensurate with the tone in which it is written, particularly when I am writing to a person like Sherry. So, this is my answer to her.

"Hi Sherry,
You are right, we have been friends for a long time, and I can understand your concerns about the trip last year. I was taking some medication, and it did cause me to do a few dumb things. I really didn't think Rudolph would follow me inside, but when he saw there was a snack, he just could not resist. The brown stains must be hoof marks, and I suggest you try RESOLVE. It is a pretty good stain remover.

I ate the whole snack because I thought it was for me. If you don't want me to eat all of it, don't put it out. To tell you the truth, it wasn't that good anyhow. If I would not have been starving, I probably would not have eaten it all.

It did hurt a little bit when you brought up the subject of my weight. I have a little trouble with my thyroid, and I have gone a little past the chubby stage. Mrs. Santa calls me her Jolly Bowl. I really don't think anyone would want a skinny Santa, though. By the way, that chair was wobbly before I sat on it. Maybe I can bring you some new furniture this year.

I will be using the door instead of the chimney. Climbing around on the roof has taken my insurance rates way up, and it gives Rudolph a panic attack when he sees me scuffing around up there. Mrs. Santa was complaining about the soot in your chimney last year. They can be cleaned, you know.

That is not Southern Comfort, I drink. It is snowball juice mixed with prune juice. It really keeps me on the go. I can see why your mother would have been concerned about losing two bottles of that stuff. That only left three for her. I am sorry you were disappointed with your gifts last year. Most people would be happy to get Castoria. If you take it, I think it would help your grouchiness. I was going to bring you a supply of Preparation H this year, but you probably wouldn't appreciate that either. I was also going to bring you a telephone book of unlisted numbers, but that is out now, too.

None of this has hurt our friendship, believe me, Sherry. I'm sure you will be surprised when you look under your Christmas tree this year. Feel free to write any time. Love, Santa."

As I have said before, I love to find humor wherever I can and I also like to make my own humor. In fact, my wife and I enjoy endless laughs and kidding around with our dearest friends Harold and Millie Bechtold. So when Millie, who has macular degeneration, decided to type a letter to Santa using her memory of the keyboard, I chose to completely reverse my usual positive attitude and have a little fun with my reply.

"Hi Millie,
I know I have taken a while to get around to answering your letter, but old Santa is having a rocky time trying to get himself in shape for the big trip. Mrs. Santa is taking on a much bigger part this year. When I showed her your letter, she could not believe how you could do this, when she found out you were doing the typing mostly from memory.

You are right—there are so many little fibs that are passed around about my reindeer. Dancer really isn't a good dancer at all. As a matter of fact, he stumbles a lot. And Prancer doesn't even know his front foot from his back foot. Comet is about to be replaced by Ajax and Vixen is a really ornery reindeer. Dasher has had so many accidents that we now call him Crasher. Cupid thinks he is a real Casanova. Donner is really a 'has-been'. And Blitzen is like a bull in a China shop. The only time Rudolph's nose is red is when he has been drinking too much snowball juice. Quite frankly, they are all a mess.

The Brownies got their calendar mixed up and thought we were making all these toys for Easter, so we are running late.

Mrs. Santa hasn't been getting much sleep, so she fell off her rocker, and I'm supposed to be running all over the world saying 'HO HO HO!' I feel like saying 'NO NO NO!'

Tomorrow I must go to see Dr. DooGood again, but I think he should change his name to Dr. DooNotTooMuchGood.

Well, I would like to write a longer letter, but quite frankly, I'm sick of this whole mess.

Say hello to that man who lives with you, whatever his name is. I understand he didn't even buy a real Christmas

tree this year. And he thinks he's so much because he has a computer. Bye now.
Love, Santa."

You have to be a very good friend to talk to someone this way. I just knew Millie would be roaring with laughter because that is the kind of person she is—one who loves to laugh and have fun.

I have delivered my very favorite talk, "Letters to Santa Claus" or "I Believe in You" more than 1,400 times since 1950. Although I have formed longstanding friendships as a result of many of those talks, I made a new friend in a different way following one of them in 2001.

That year, a news reporter from the Lancaster Intelligencer Journal attended one of my talks and wrote an article about it for his newspaper. It hit the Associated Press wire service and almost immediately my telephone started to ring with calls from radio and television stations all over the country.

One of those calls came from Ted Koppel's "Nightline." A crew of five people from the show spent a total of eight hours on the story. First they spent three hours in my hometown of Hanover, Pennsylvania, and then they came to our home in Lancaster, Pennsylvania, and spent five hours doing interviews and videotaping. They could not have been a nicer, more professional group of people.

The results of those interviews took place on Christmas Eve, in a short segment on the television show, "Nightline." As you might suspect, that generated more letters from other parts of the United States. However, that is not how I made a new friend.

The friendship was formed after one of the "Nightline" photographers named George told me his mother-in-law, Joane, was dealing with a serious illness and was not dealing with it in a very good way. The problem was that she was so used to giving all of her life, she found it very difficult to receive when other people offered help. George thought it might be a good idea if I sent a letter from Santa Claus that could perhaps lift her spirits.

This idea appealed to me immediately, and I asked him a few questions about Joane. I wanted to know about her immediate family, her personality, her sense of humor and her favorite foods. It just so happened that two of her three favorite foods, potato chips and chocolate, are made in Pennsylvania -- chocolates in Hershey, and potato chips in Hanover.

You can imagine Joane's surprise when a box of Utz's potato chips and a box of Hershey's chocolates arrived from Santa Claus in time for her birthday. Joane and I kept in touch for several years and each holiday and birthday I sent her potato chips and chocolates. Here is the latest letter I wrote to her.

"Dear Joane,
You know, it has been a long time since I heard from you,
so I decided to take a little time from my 'little friends' and
write to one of my new friends. I want this to be a little
Christmas present for you. I have something else on the way
that I think will be a taste of goodness. I am not going to
tell you what it is, because it is a surprise. I can tell you one
thing—it is not a crab cake and it isn't even chocolate—and
I know you like both of those things, don't you?

Joane, I know you are going through a rough time right
now and sometimes that happens to all of us. Believe
me, old Santa has had a taste of that recently, too. I can
tell you something—the one thing I always hold onto is
HOPE. Let me tell you what we do up here. When one of us
is going through some real struggles, I call a meeting with
Mrs. Santa and all the Brownies and we have what we call
a ring of prayer. Believe me, when I get all of us praying
for the same thing, there is a lot of power. We never give
up on anything. My Brownies have a saying and it is, 'It is
always too soon to quit.'

You have been giving to others for many, many years
because I know you believe it is better to give than to
receive. But do you know what, Joane? We must be willing
to let those around us who love us, do their share of
giving because that's what they want to do. I am sure I
am speaking for your daughter, Jennifer, your son-in-law,
George, and your two grandchildren, Sarah and Julie Anne.
You will always be sweet Noni to them. I know your son,
John, is at a distance but I am sure he, too, wants to give

some back. I know you aren't asking my advice, but I am going to give some on my own. Mrs. Santa and I have always put our lives in God's hands because ultimately we know He controls everything. So, we have peace of mind. I know you believe in the same Book as I do. There is such strength in prayer.

Well, Joane, I hear Mrs. Santa giving me a whistle from the other room and I know what that means. She told me she is making me some chocolate peanut butter fudge and I think she wants me to sample it. Everyone up here is wishing you a blessed and joyous holiday season, and I'd like you to sit back and drink in the love from all of those around you who think that you are one precious lady.
Love, Santa.

P.S. Be on the lookout for that little surprise. It is being selected with care and love."

The year following the Nightline interview, my wife, Gloria, arranged an absolute surprise 80th birthday party for me with approximately 160 people in attendance. The last guests to arrive, from Virginia, were Joane, her daughter, Jennifer, and her son-in-law, George, along with their children, Sarah and Julie Anne. What a beautiful surprise for me to meet this lovely lady, along with her family. I guess you might say that was the "crowning jewel" of the guest list that evening.

Chapter Three

"Little" Children with "Big" Hearts (Including Letters from 9/11)

There is something about giving that creates a warm feeling inside—not just because the adage says, "It's better to give than to receive," but simply because there is something special about how you feel when you give. It doesn't mean we shouldn't like to receive, because it is also important to be gracious when receiving a gift. If we aren't, we take away the joy of the person who so willingly wants to display love in that way.

I've often marveled at the way many children are so willing to share what they have with others. That unselfishness is such a beautiful quality. I admire that trait, and I think parents are wise if they teach that early in a child's life.

Keith and Maria are a great example of this kind of parental leadership. Each Christmas, they ask their daughter, Hana, to give three of her new presents to a child who is in need. She loves doing it and does it very willingly. However, it surprises her parents when she chooses one of her nicest presents to give away. I believe Hana knows the true meaning of Christmas.

For me, although I have always loved the work I have done in my professional life, no job has ever been more rewarding than my "ministry" of writing Santa letters to children. I receive no monetary reward for this, but it has always filled my heart with joy.

I think people leave a huge void in their lives if they never experience the giving spirit. It's like being in a cold, dark church with stained glass windows and no sun shining through.

Although people sometimes believe that little children just write letters with long lists of what they want for Christmas, that is often not the case. I can't say that I've never gotten any like that, but it's surprising how few I do get of that nature. Instead, I get letters asking that I remember the poor children all over the world.

Often, little children are affected and responsive to events that happen around the world. For instance, following the September 11, 2001, horrific tragedy in this country, I received many letters from children asking me to make sure the families and children affected by this life-changing event were taken care of. It is so touching to hear children reaching out to other children and other families.

These are a few excerpts to give you some idea of the tone of many others I received.

"Dear Santa,
I want you to make sure all the victim's families from
September 11th have a good Christmas.
Sincerely, Lauren."

"Dear Santa,
And give lots of stuff to the poor kids and the kids that lost
their parents in Sep. 11th.
Sincerely, Kenny."

"Dear Santa,
For Christmas I wish you would get New York children toys.
Your friend, Ashley."

"Dear Santa Claus,
I hope you will bring us a lot of toy's. We were good and
kind to others people and I think that that is a nise thing
to do don't - you? Well I do and that is good. And so are
you. You are good to us and thats a good thing that you
are. Mary Christmas and a Happy New Year!
Love, Traci."

"Dear Santa Claus,
My name is Spencer. What I want for Christmas is NO
MORE WAR!!
Love, Spencer."

You might be interested to know that Spencer, from Denver, Colorado, had this very short letter printed in red crayon with letters about two inches in height. Strong emotion was written all over that letter of few words.

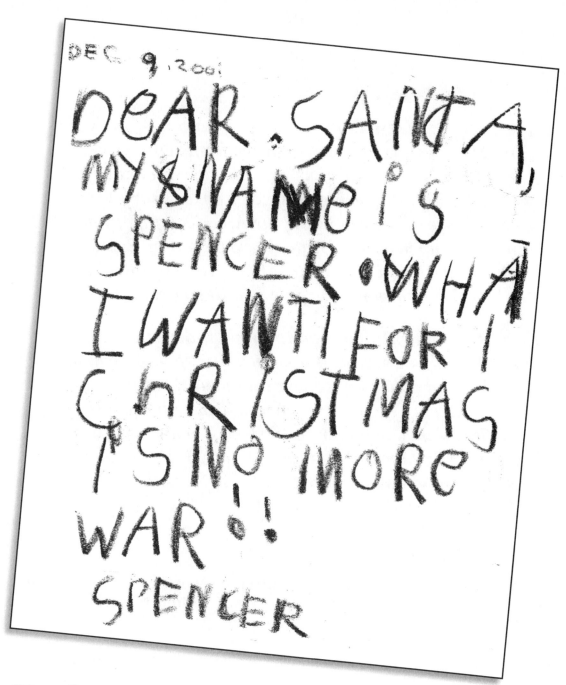

DEC 9, 2001

DEAR SANTA,
MY NAME IS
SPENCER. WHA
I WANT FOR
CHRISTMAS
IS NO MORE
WAR!!

SPENCER

"Dear Santa,
I hope you and Mrs. Claus have a wonderful Christmas
and will pray with me for world peace.
Thank you, Sydney."

My answers to these little children with big hearts always require as much sensitivity as I can muster. I want to make certain to acknowledge their hurts and their concerns, as you can see by the following responses.

"We were so pleased to hear about your wish for a good Christmas for the victims' families from September 11th. I'm sure they will be a little sad, but they probably feel good about all the caring they got from so many people like you. We have been flying the American flag from all of our cabins up here. The Brownies went out on September 12th and put them up. We are all so proud of the kindness that has been shown by people just like you.

It was so thoughtful of you to think of the children in New York. You can be sure we have been thinking of them often, too. Rudolph was very concerned about these little ones in New York when he was mapping out the trip, so he made sure they were one of our early stops. I want you to know that we will have lots of toys for the children in New York. We want to put some smiles on those faces that have had reasons to be sad."

Following a short paragraph acknowledging their concerns, I immediately shift the mood to a much lighter state by telling the children about some of the "fun stuff" from the North Pole happenings. The greatest portion of the letter is purposefully written to lighten their hearts and transfer their minds from the reality to the fantasy to help them get beyond their sadness.

The following answer was to the child who remembered the children in Afghanistan.

"It was so thoughtful of you to remember the little boys and girls in Afghanistan. You can be sure I won't forget them. You are so lucky to be living in the USA, aren't you?

President Bush came up here last week to see how we get so much done in so little time."

To Spencer, who requested no more war for Christmas, I answered with the following words:

"It sounds like you only have one thing you want for Christmas and that is no war. I can certainly understand that wish. It may help you to know that we are all praying up here for world peace. The Brownie Chorus has been singing 'God Bless America', too. Did you know that we have a game up here called 'Tug of Love' instead of 'Tug of War'? We also have Brownies named Eeeny, Miney and Moe. We don't have any Meanies up here."

To many of the children who were concerned about other children who may have had a parent who died, I answered,

"I think it is nice that you remembered the boys and girls who may have lost their parents on September 11th. We are keeping them in our prayers. I am getting lots of letters from other children just like you. I can see that you have been taught to care and share."

Children have such big hearts, don't they? I think it is important at times like these to let them know that we recognize the good in them. I tried to do that in this next answer.

"I see you didn't forget anyone in your family when you wrote your letter. That is nice to be thinking of others, especially the people who lost their family members in that terrible tragedy. You can be sure those people will be first on my list because they need me the most. I am sure you can understand that."

As I mentioned, letters related to the 9/11 tragedy are not the only ones I have received from children expressing their concern for others. As you can see by the following letters, children often reveal their loving and giving spirits when they write to Santa.

"Dear Santa,
Maybe if you have the time, a gameboy advanced. (I might give my regular gameboy to my sister.) For Frosty, a dog couch and please, the biggest bone you have and some treats. For my sister a Diva Star and some barbie dolls. For my brother some gameboy games and Harry Potter cards. For my Dad a lot of three Stooges stuff (he's a really big fan!) And for my mom candells and puzzles. I hope you have a very good Christmas and thank you.
From, Zach."

"Dear Santa,
Will you please give me a warm coat for Christmas so I can give it to my friend Ariel? She does not have a warm coat to wear. You are such a kind person.
From your friend, Stephanie."

"Dear Santa,
I hope you are ready for Christmas. This year I would like a mountain bike. Because I am giving my bike to a girl who

dose not have a bike. This year I would like it if my Aunt
Debby and my cousins Lindsay and Candice cold come
back form Florida to visit.
Love, Kendall."

"Dear Santa,
I hope I can have a puppy for my neighbor because her dog
was run over yesterday. I hope I can have a toy car and
some things for other people. I hope I can have some money
for my grandma and grandpa. I hope I can get some toys
for other kids. I hope I can get some money for the pour.
Your friend, Christian."

In her letter, Jamie displays that wonderful caring attitude in quite a different way.

"Dear Santa,
How are you? How is Mrs. Clause? Are the raindeer ok?
Are the elves ok? Santa I think I have been a good girl.
The reson I think that is because I cared for my garden and
loved all the nature in my backyard and cared for it all. If
I was mean or creal to something tell me what I did and
tell me what I did it to. I promise I will never do it again. I
have loved everyone and tried to make everyone happy."

She also includes a list for her mother and her father, which tells me she cares not only for her garden but for her parents, too.

Abby warmed my heart when she wrote to me after Christmas.

"Dear Santa,
Why, why am I writing to you after Christmas? Well, I'll
tell you why. You probably get letters that always say, I
want, I want, I want. Now I am saying. Thank you, thank
you, thank you."

Isn't that precious?

I am always heartened by the depth of some children's understanding of the importance of giving. Hunter's mother wrote a letter for him and shared the special traits of her little boy. For such a small boy, he has already learned so much about what giving really means. I would have to say he knows the Spirit of Giving from the bottom of his heart. I want you to hear my response, which will let you know why my heart was warmed and why I had a tear in my eye as I answered his letter.

"Hi Hunter,
I can't remember getting a letter that made me feel so good
about the things I read. First of all, let me say this to you.
You are one unusual boy and without a doubt, one of the
most caring I know. I think it is so good of you to share
your allowance with charitable causes. Certainly St. Jude's
is one of them because they do so much good for little
children. I also know how hard you work when you stand
outside and ring the Salvation Army bell because it can be
very chilly sometimes."

Like parents, teachers can also set great examples for children. In fact, it is often said that we "teach by example," and children are apt to follow our example even more than our advice.

One exceptional teacher who immediately comes to my mind when I think of leading by example is Miss Amanda Light, who taught Kindergarten at the Rainbow Learning Center in Lebanon, Pennsylvania.

Miss Amanda first learned about me from the mother of one of her students, Michelle Miller. Mrs. Miller's daughter, Megan, wrote to me individually, but then Mrs. Miller put the bug in Miss Amanda's ear that perhaps she might want to make a class project out of this.

Mrs. Miller was aware of my birthday, October 15, and passed along this information to Miss Amanda. Lo and behold, a few days before my birthday I received this huge birthday card made by Miss Amanda and her students. The card must have been about four feet by three feet, and all the little ones signed it and put their own letters with it. Part of their letters included a drawing of a birthday cake, which each child colored with his or her own style.

I wanted to be sure there was a special answer for this unique birthday remembrance, so I assigned a Brownie to each one of the students. Just to give you an example of the special names I come up with for the Brownies, here is the list for this particular class:

Bradley	Happy	Evan	Dale
Cade	Peppy	Kaden	Misty
Carter	Pippy	Katie	Popcorn
Christian	Hoppy	Makenna	Scotty
Andrew	Jingles	Montana	Bronko
Carter L.	Jazzy	Nicholas	Sparky
Dagon	Winky	Sam	Sandy
Dru	Dapper	Sarah	Sadie
Elizabeth	Lizzy	Hallie	Boomer
Christella	Puffy	Megan	Mickey
JR.	Jake	Zachary	Zeke
Makendra	Mac	Ziven	Ziggy
Janelle	Donny		

Before Christmas, I received another big envelope from Miss Amanda's class. This time, she had prepared a customized form for each child to fill out with his or her name, an individually assigned Brownie's name, and what each child would leave for Santa's snack on Christmas Eve.

One of the things that surprised me was the variety of snacks they selected. Most of the time children leave cookies and milk for me, and for Rudolph, they leave apples or carrots. In this case, I noticed that as they filled out their forms, they were leaving Santa things like French fries, green beans, fried chicken and mashed potatoes.

This aroused my curiosity and I ended up calling Miss Amanda to see if she had an explanation for this. She just chuckled and told me they must have come up with these unusual items because they had written the letters right after Thanksgiving. Apparently they had lots of leftovers!

Several weeks later, I called Miss Amanda again – this time to see if she would be interested in attending my "Santa Claus Talk." I was planning to give the talk to the Cornwall Manor Retirement Community, located only a few miles from the Rainbow Learning Center. Miss Amanda accepted my invitation, and she arrived with a beautiful, framed, color photograph of the students, flanked by her and her assistant, Miss Janice. This was such a wonderful surprise and I was touched by it.

Along came Easter time and a "Priority" mail package came into the post office addressed to Santa Claus with the Rainbow Learning Center on the return address. Well, I couldn't wait to open it to see what was inside. Yes, I am like a little kid when it comes to receiving surprise packages, too.

What a delight to find inside the box a decorated plastic egg from each of the children and from Miss Amanda and Miss Janice. The eggs were nestled in a bed of green straw. Inside each egg was the name of the child or teacher who decorated it along with a little fuzzy baby chick. No, the chicks weren't real, but they were cute. Mrs. Santa and I had the biggest chuckle over these very special Easter eggs. I included the following reply in my surprise package of chocolate Easter egg lollipops to them.

"Hi Boys and Girls,
You are so full of surprises there at the Rainbow Learning Center. I think we might ask Miss Amanda to come up here sometime to our Christmas Creative Center and bring some of her new ideas along. She and Mrs. Santa would get along really great because Mrs. Santa has that creative touch, too.

When your box of decorated eggs came, I called a special meeting of all the Brownies and shared my surprise with them. A lot of them were pretty busy decorating eggs for the big Easter Egg Roll up here on Merry Mountain.

I thought you might be interested in knowing who worked on our little surprise we are sending you. Two of my Brownies in the Candy Shop, Rollo and Reese, made the chocolate lollipops. Mrs. Santa and two of her Brownies in the Surprise Shop, Ticker and Taper, wrapped the lollipops and put the stickers on. Buttons and Bows put the ribbons on because they are used to that since they work with Mrs. Santa in the Doll Shop. As you can see, I am sending my heart to all of you if you look closely at your lollipops.

Of course, each of your special-assigned Brownies wanted to make a label with your name and theirs on it, so you will see what a nice job they did. They are so clever. They could hardly wait for everything to be finished since their label was the last thing to put on.

Mrs. Santa and I have voted Miss Amanda and Miss Janice 'TEACHERS OF THE YEAR.' We allowed each of the Brownies to have a vote and they all voted for the two of them.

Mrs. Santa got me the biggest egg I have ever seen and she told me it took a pint of ink to color it. I asked her where she got it, and she told me it was an ostrich egg. Maybe Miss Amanda can show you a picture of an ostrich. It has a big long neck, long legs, big eyes, and a very little head. I thought you might like to see a picture of the beautiful egg, Mrs. Santa painted. She is so good at this stuff. Isn't it pretty?

Well, I guess I had better go now. Rudolph just stopped by to tell me they are ready for me to look at the map they have for the big Egg Roll. He and the other reindeer set up the course because they are used to planning. They have had lots of practice mapping out our big trip at Christmas, so this will be a piece of cake for him and his team.

Be good to each other and be good for Miss Amanda and Miss Janice. I know you will be good for your mommies and daddies, too. That always makes us smile up here. Bye now. Love, Santa."

With the devotion of time and care given by Miss Amanda to the various letters and cards sent to Santa, I'm sure you can see why I feel Miss Amanda has so many of the attributes I appreciate in teachers.

Over the years, I have heard from many, many teachers across the country. There have been letters from Pennsylvania, New Jersey, Virginia, Maine, North Carolina, Nebraska and Maryland. Many teachers send letters every year, telling me about their first grade or kindergarten class. Most teachers also include individual letters from each of the children.

One of the most unusual letters I ever received from a teacher came from first-grade teacher Jeannie Boltz from Pine Street Elementary School in Palmyra, Pennsylvania. When she found out about my project, she wrote me a short letter tinged with disbelief. She also had all 34 of her students write a letter to Santa.

Her letter said only this:

"Well, Santa, if you really do answer letters, we'll take one."

I thought, "Oh boy, she really sounds excited." In my effort to prove to her that I am for real, I sat down and typed a two-page letter to Jeannie and her class. I assigned a personal Brownie to each one of the children and told them each Brownie's name. However, I didn't receive a reply from her – that is until three days before Valentine's Day.

Inside a manila envelope were valentines made for me by each one of the children. The cover letter was typical for Jeannie and had few words. It said,

"Well, we know what you do at Christmas time, Santa Claus, but what are you doing in February?"

I couldn't help but say to myself, "Man, this lady is tough!" Nobody ever posed that question before. So I asked myself, "What am I doing up here in February?" I couldn't just tell her I was lying around getting fat drinking snowball juice, so I had to make up something.

The wheels in my head started turning and I said to myself, "You know, Grover, you have not been stumped heretofore. You had better come up with something."

On my way to lunch, I took a shortcut through a local Five and 10 store and as I passed the candy counter, I noticed these little candy hearts—you know the ones that have messages on them? "Kiss me." "Hug me." "Run away with me." "I love you."

Well, the ladies behind the counter were making necklaces out of these hearts. And then it hit me. I thought, "That's what we're doing up here!" So I went over to the counter and said to the lady, "I'll have six strands of those hearts."

I let my imagination take over while I ate lunch, and when I returned to the office, I sat down at the typewriter and typed,

"Jeannie, you asked me what the Brownies were doing up here in February. Well, they are making love beads in February and they want you to have the first six strands!"

Then I went on to tell her about the Sweetheart Hop and the Sock Hop we were having. I told her we were giving prizes to the Brownies that had the best socks and the one that won had his socks painted on his feet and ankles. I told her Rudolph was going over to the Crippled Children's Hospital and was taking the children for rides on the sled.

I didn't hear back from Jeannie Boltz, of course. However, three days before Easter, in came another manila envelope. All of the children in her class had signed the enclosed cards, and the cover letter from Jeannie Boltz said,

"Dear Santa Claus—Don't even take the time to answer this letter. I know how busy you must be up there laying eggs!"

Well, I wasn't laying eggs at Easter time, but I did have an interesting experience with one teacher from Kreutz Elementary School in Hallem, Pennsylvania. One of her students asked if I knew the Easter Bunny. I thought if anyone should know the Easter Bunny, I should. So I wrote back,

"As a matter of fact, I do know the Easter Bunny and I am going to see the Easter Bunny in about two days."

This was right around the Easter season, so I went to Sauder Egg Company in Lititz, Pennsylvania, and bought three-dozen colored hard-boiled eggs. Then I made a trip to the school in Hallem.

I waited until the children were at recess, and I put the three-dozen colored eggs with a letter from Santa on the teacher's desk. I don't know how she explained it to her students, but I'll bet those kids were convinced that I knew the Easter Bunny!

Another top-notch schoolteacher is Mrs. Beth Basehore. That was made evident by the time she must have taken to prepare a beautiful booklet as a class project. You have to have a lot of patience, love and creativity to design a booklet.

Mrs. Basehore is another one of the teachers who has written to me for many years. I hope you enjoy the following answer, which I wrote to her class.

"Hi Boys and Girls,
I just knew I was going to hear from you this year. Mrs.
Basehore is one of my favorite teachers and she is so
dependable. I am sure she is teaching you to be the same
way. If you tell someone you are going to do something, then
you must do it. We just can't make promises we don't keep.

It was very kind of you to thank me for your presents last
year. Believe me, we enjoy making them as much as you

enjoy getting them. We do work hard and all we ask is that you take good care of them. When you are finished playing with them, pick them up and put them away.

I don't think you got any snow there in Silver Spring, but I do know you got some very cold weather and some high winds. I know some of you would like to see some snow soon because you like to play in it and build snowmen. I think you ought to build some snow-women, too, when you get enough snow. The Brownies always have a snowman and snow-woman building contest. You can't believe how well they dress them. Two of Mrs. Santa's helpers in the Doll Workshop give them some pretty good advice. Their names are Frizzy and Lizzy.

I sure did appreciate it when you said, 'We love you, Santa!' Nobody can get too much love and I am sending you as much as you can send through the mail. We do a lot of hugging up here because we like each other, but it also helps to keep us warm. The first part is the most important part.

Now let me answer your questions. Rudolph and his team pull the sleigh and they make miracle magic movements and it is really faster than flying. My whole trip is just one big miracle after another. Keeping my nose warm is one of my biggest problems. Mrs. Santa is working on knitting me a wrap-around for my face. I think it will be ready before my big trip. Rudolph and I will be making a practice run, so we might come by your school and see how you have your room decorated. Rudolph hopes you have a picture of him. He is such a great reindeer. He takes care of his reindeer almost as well as Mrs. Basehore takes care of you, and you know how good that is. He even eats some of the same things you eat, like apples, carrots and ice cream.

We have some Brownies who make a lot of our decorations up here and we have a Bell Barn. The Brownies make all of the bells for my reindeer. The Brownie in charge there is named Ringer. I wish you could see how he decorates my cabin.

The Brownies are very proud of my sleigh and they make sure it is always polished and ready to go on a moment's notice. Each year they add a new coat of paint and Rackem, Packem, and Stackem are always the sled loaders. They use turtle wax to make the sleigh shiny.

I don't have any trouble getting toys for you because I have lots and lots of Brownies who work day and night to make sure I have enough for my big trip. We can't always make everything that every boy and girl wants, but we try to be as fair as we can be. Another thing you may not know is that we work all year round.

Not all of my elves have pointy toes and ears. They are just like everyone else. Even in your class, some of you have more pointed ears and noses than others.

It is not hard to find reindeer up here at the North Pole. We have more reindeer than you have horses and cows down there. They love the cold weather, and up here we don't allow guns so nobody can shoot them. Did you know that Rudolph now has a second team and a third team just in case something happens to one of his regular team members?

My home up here at the North Pole is as far north as you can get and it is about as cold as you can get. The South Pole is pretty cold, too, and some of my Brownies do come from the South Pole to help out during our busiest season.

I expect you to be good boys and girls just like you said you are. I want you to be nice to each other and to Mrs. Basehore, too. She is such a nice lady. I used to call your teacher Bouncy Beth because she was so lively. I thought I would like to send all of you a special award since you have been so good.

Well, boys and girls, I'll be seeing all of you Christmas Eve even though you won't be seeing me. You'll know I was there when you wake up Christmas morning, though! Love, Santa."

After Santa and Mrs. Santa appeared on the Nightline Christmas Eve special in 2001, an onslaught of letters came in from various locations in Nebraska, including Mrs. Cindy's class.

As you read my answer, you will learn about some very special helpers they had in writing their letters. Santa thought their letters showed the spirit of teamwork. This is another example of teaching children the importance of giving their time for others.

In this world today, there is so much evidence of the good in kids, if you look for it. I hope you enjoy reading my answer to Mrs. Cindy's class in Nebraska.

"Hi Boys and Girls,
Your letters are so special this year, and I want to thank all of the 7th graders who helped write your letters. What a neat thing for them to do. You can be sure I will remember them, too, on Christmas Eve. After I read your letters, I gave them to Mrs. Santa so she could see how many good things you are doing like making your beds and helping out at home.

If all of you leave cookies and milk like you say you are going to do, I had better bring some back to Mrs. Santa or she will be upset. I thought it was neat that some of you drew Christmas trees and decorations on the backs of your letters. I want to give you a special award for this. This is our 'NICE JOB' award.

Don't you worry about Rudolph getting sick. He has never been sick for any of our trips because he keeps himself in tip-top shape. He works out at the Reindeer Ranch every day and, believe it or not, he can do 50 push-ups with his front feet alone. Most of his team members are up to about 25 push-ups, but they all want to see if they can catch up to Rudolph.

We also have a special Brownie vet up here by the name of Dr. DooMuch, and he spends practically all of his time taking care of the reindeer. Rudolph has a second and a third team, you know, just in case someone would get sick. One time Dancer got the reindeer rash and we did substitute Singer for him. Dancer was so disappointed that he had to miss the trip, but it was for his own good.

The Brownies are having a big party for the crippled children at the hospital. Rudolph and his team are going to take some of them on sled rides and Mrs. Santa is going to take some of her cheerleaders to do some stunts for them. I am surprised that Mrs. Santa can still fit into her leotards, but she can! She is working on a workout book now and it is called 'Make the Most of What you Have.' She is really into this hot yoga now and she can almost touch her head with her toes. I wouldn't even think of trying that.

We have a new mall up here now and they call it the Frozen Mile Shopping Mall and we have a lot of fast food restaurants. One of them specializes in snowball soup and another in spaghetti pie. We have a Polar Pizza and a Popsicle Palace.

Boys and girls, I can tell you one thing. We are going to make Omaha, Nebraska, one of our early stops this year. Some of my members of the Brownie football team like the Nebraska Cornhuskers. I do think they ought to send their quarterback up here to our football training school. The Brownie Bombers' quarterbacks are Bullseye and Laser.

By the way, we all think it would be good to give those 7th graders an award for being such a big help to you in writing your letters. This award is for being so 'FANTASTIC' in the way they helped all of you. I hope you will show it to them and tell them I said they are not only 'FANTASTIC,' but they are also 'SANTASTIC!'

I guess I had better wrap this up now and head over to the Wrapping Cabin. When I say Wrapping Cabin, I mean wrapping presents, not that funny rapping music stuff.

That hurts my ears. You be good for Mrs. Cindy because I know she is good to you. Why don't you give her a big hug for me? See you Christmas Eve.
Love, Santa."

As you can see, there was much love and care from the older students as they sat down and helped the little ones with their letters to Santa. I would say these 7th graders had big hearts, too, wouldn't you?

Following will be one of my answers to a class that also made a booklet for me as a class project. It was beautifully decorated as many of them are. The booklet was from the Hildebrandt Learning Center in Lancaster, Pennsylvania. I will first tell you that each child had an individual page with a drawing and one question for Santa. I'm sure it took some real thought to develop.

"Hi Boys and Girls,
HI-HO, HI-HO, Once again, you get the prize for the prettiest and most original book of letters! When it came in I just had to call a meeting of the Brownies and show it to them. I knew they would want to see it, and they went back to work happier than ever after they saw your letters. They will probably work twice as hard now because they are twice as happy.

As always, I am going to answer every question you asked. Erin, it is hard to know how many reindeer I really have. I know Rudolph has his first, second, and third teams, so that is 24 right there. Then there is Rudolph and his wife, Pinky. There are also a lot of herds of reindeer up here just like you have a lot of herds of cows down there.

Jessica, I sure do give people shirts for Christmas if that is what they want and need. Jason, the polar bears you talk about do not need warm places to stay. They dig holes in the snow and sometimes they lay on the ice and do ice fishing.

Eliza, snow comes from rain that is frozen up in the sky before it hits the ground. You certainly got a lot of it a couple of weeks ago. Charlotte, Rudolph's nose gets redder and brighter when we are on the big trip. It helps light the way!

Kyana, we make our own candy up here. We have candy shops the whole way up and down Candy Lane. We make our own peppermint canes, peppermint patties, peanut butter fudge, marshmallows, white chocolate, and lots more! We have 143 different flavors of jelly beans.

Samantha, I eat a lot of cookies because a lot of people leave them for me to eat. I would eat candy or potato chips or apples or cheese or carrots or anything else they would leave for me. I am not picky. Emma, I give out toys because I like to put smiles on the faces of little boys and girls. Doesn't that make you smile?

Jeffrey, most of my Brownies, or what you call elves, come from the South Pole and the North Pole. Down South they are called Greenies, but we make Brownies out of them. Alima, we have lots of balls to play with. We have rubber balls, beach balls, baseballs, golf balls, footballs, basketballs, and most of all—SNOWBALLS! Mrs. Santa even makes soup out of snowballs.

Sarah, our reindeer grow up right here. This is reindeer country. We don't have a lot of cows up here, but we sure do have reindeer. Did you know that reindeer give milk? Adrienne, do we ever have cats! I can't even begin to count the number of cats. Since you asked about them, I thought I would send along a picture of one of Mrs. Santa's cats. Her name is Fleece. I must admit, she is pretty, but she sure is lazy.

Haley, my Brownies, or elves, have workshops up here and they learn to make toys and games of all kinds as they are growing up. Not only can they do one job, they can do about three or four jobs. The harder they work, the louder they sing.

Jonny, even though you read this in books, I don't use those chimneys anymore. I have a master key and I can get into any of your doors. Also, it is safer. Emily, you know I certainly do give presents. All I ask is that you take good care of them. We work hard and we want you to put them away when you are finished playing with them.

And finally, Elizabeth, I don't know what to tell you my favorite food is. I like almost every food that is good for you. I eat a lot of seafood and I eat lots of vegetables and fruit. I especially like spinach, broccoli, beans and salads. However, I also like snowball sundaes, polar peach pie and frozen whoopie pies.

Well, I think I have answered all your questions. Now I want to ask you a few questions. Are you being good for your teacher? Are you saying your prayers? Are you doing nice things for each other? Are you sharing and are you helping your moms and dads around the house? If the answer is 'Yes,' that will make me very, very happy. I am looking forward to seeing every one of you on Christmas Eve. Bye now.
 Love, Santa."

I'll bet most of you can remember specific teachers from your years of learning. In many cases, it will be a kindergarten or first grade teacher, rather than a teacher from later in our school years. That is because we were having so much fun learning, and learning should be fun.

I'd like to think I was able to teach children something about giving when I taught ballroom dancing classes many years ago. I enlisted the help of the executive director of the Hanover YWCA in getting the students for the children's class. I said I preferred to teach boys and girls between the ages of 10 and 14 so they could learn to dance before their junior or senior proms in high school. It's no fun to stand around while everyone else is having fun dancing.

When I held my first class, there were 16 girls and two boys. It was not exactly the ratio I was hoping for. Apparently, the boys of that age had other interests. However, after I gave the two boys a "pep talk" and showed them how much fun it was to hold the girls while they were dancing, I asked them to talk with some of their buddies about coming to the remainder of the classes. Obviously my "pep talk" worked because in the following sessions, I had 16 girls and 14 boys in attendance.

In the process of teaching them to dance, I also instructed the boys to be polite and have good manners when asking a girl to dance. I told them to compliment the girl about her nice dress or pleasant smile or say something else praiseworthy.

On the final evening of our class, I saw this little boy, Jimmy, walk up to a little girl named Sally and ask for a dance. Both of them were a little rotund and suited to be anything but good dance partners. However, they really seemed to be enjoying their dancing.

The Nickelodeon played 10 records and it seemed like they continued dancing even through the change of the records. Finally, when the last record played and the music stopped, I watched the two of them walk over to the chairs on the side of the room.

Sally kind of plopped down on the chair, and I saw Jimmy looking rather uncomfortable. He moved his hands in and out of his pockets, fiddled with his tie and seemed to be in some kind of torment.

I had told all the boys that they should say something nice to the girl at the end of the dance. For instance, "You have a nice red dress on," or "I like the red bow in your hair." It was obvious to me as I watched Jimmy that he was trying to think of something nice to say to Sally. Finally, he pulled his hands out of his pockets and pulled himself up to his full height. And then he blurted out, "You sweat less than any fat girl I ever danced with."

Certainly Jimmy could have said something more complimentary, but Sally seemed to accept it in the spirit in which it was given. I think the two of them had a great evening! It was one of my most amusing examples of teaching.

Chapter Four
Happy Thoughts–Happy Faces

When you think of it, a smile doesn't require any special talent. All that is really needed is a happy heart. As adults, I think it is easy for us to plant the seed of a smile in our children. The key is a happy home, and giving children an environment that lends itself well to happy hearts.

One man with a happy heart, whom I often think about even though he is no longer with us, is Bill Brownfield, the author of the Jaycee Creed. The words in the Creed are what all Jaycees are to live by. The first line of that Creed says, "Faith in God gives meaning and purpose to human life." The last line of the Creed says, "Service to humanity is the best work of life."

I was fortunate to be sitting beside Bill on a plane trip to a Jaycee convention on the west coast late in the 1950's, when I was serving as vice president of the United States Jaycees. I knew Bill well enough to talk to him about his struggle with multiple sclerosis.

In the course of our conversation, I said to him, "Bill, I don't think I have ever seen you at any of our national meetings when you did not have a smile on your face. How in the world can you do that, given the fact you are dealing with a disease like multiple sclerosis?" With that same smile on his face, he looked at me and said, "Grover, I don't know how much you know about multiple sclerosis, but the disease has never reached my heart. My heart is happy about that and it tells my face, and then my face smiles."

Bill handled nearly a lifetime of having multiple sclerosis and yet managed to give away smiles to everyone else. There should be more Bill Brownfield's in this world— not stricken with disease, but with an attitude like his. A smile doesn't cost anything, and the investment and dividend can be very rewarding.

I wish it were possible to show you the smiles of the more than 100,000 children who have written to me over the years, but obviously that is out of the question. What I can do is show you a representative collection of some of those children in the following pages. Try looking at all these happy faces and tell me it doesn't bring a smile to your face.

Miss Amanda's Class

Chapter Five
The Imagination Inside Santa's Loop

There should be no age limit for imagination. It's easy when we are children because we have no inhibitions and no one to put restrictions on our imaginative thinking. However, as we grow older, we often think of too many reasons why something cannot be done rather than striking out to do it.

Entrepreneurs are people who still allow those creative juices to flow. That's good. Personally, I would be at a tremendous loss if I had not kept my childlike imagination. In order to write back to the children who write to Santa, I must think on their level. That makes the whole process fun – and funny.

I don't mind admitting that when I am dictating my answers to Mrs. Santa, sometimes we both just sit back and laugh out loud. A sense of humor is such a good remedy for easing any kind of stress. That's another lesson all adults could learn.

Since you are reading this book, you deserve to be "inside Santa's loop." Let me bring you up to date on some of the things we "do" up here at the North Pole.

Maybe this will answer some of the many questions we get from children who write letters to Santa Claus.

What does Mrs. Santa do?

Many youngsters are interested in what Mrs. Santa does. Needless to say, she is a very busy lady, and I mean all year round. I certainly don't know what I would do without her. Most people never get to know Mrs. Santa very closely, but after you read this you will feel like she is one of your closest friends. Mrs. Santa helps me a great deal in all of my activities and she certainly is my closest friend.

I want to tell you just some of the things she does on a regular basis. She loves to have fun, and every time we have square dancing up here with the Brownies, she loves to do-si-do. She is also in charge of the Brownie cheerleaders who cheer at all of the Brownies' games and she calls them the Snowbelles. I was so surprised when I saw just how many different exercises she does with those Brownies. She is so spry.

Mrs. Santa is also into music. She leads the Brownie Choir and plays the piano and organ at church. She teaches dance of all kinds, including toe, tap and ballet. Because she was eating a little too much a time ago, she was having trouble getting into her tutu. She did, however, make herself a four-four and wore that for a while. Happily she lost some weight and now is back into her tutu.

During the summertime, Mrs. Santa teaches kindergarten. She believes we should never stop learning and the earlier we start, the better off we will be. Once in a while when we have a little time we like to play Scrabble. That keeps us up to date on our mental word exercises.

Of course, Mrs. Santa does a lot of sewing since she is in charge of the Doll Workshop up here. She has plenty of help and has trained some of the Brownies so well that they can run the Doll Workshop when she is doing something else. She does some baking and specializes in soft sugar cookies and blueberry muffins. She knows how much I like them and she is always trying some new things because she knows I am "snack-happy."

Mrs. Santa loves to read and sometimes she is reading three or four books at one time. I don't know how in the world she keeps the stories straight in her mind. Mrs. Santa is also a whiz on the computer and she is always doing special projects for other people— like making up wedding invitations or graduation announcements. She is so creative.

She has been working out in the fitness center a lot more lately. She found that is a good way to keep in shape so she never grows out of that tutu again. She especially likes to do that Bikram yoga because it is done in a hot room. It's about 110 degrees and she just loves it. She says it makes her joints feel good. I guess she likes to get out of the cold, but I don't think I could stand that much heat. I will just stick by my fireplace. That's enough for me.

One of the things many people don't know about Mrs. Santa is how generous she is with her time. She organized a humming choir with the Brownies because some of them couldn't remember the words. She didn't want them to feel left out.

Not many people know this, but I also teach dancing and have for a long time. I have some special dances I do like the Santa Shuffle, the Santa Swing, the Santa Shimmy and the Santa Shake. I remember one time Mrs. Santa tried to do the Santa Shake and she almost threw her hip out of joint, so she hasn't tried it since that time.

Mrs. Santa and I have a TV program called Santa's Showcase. We usually have a special guest every week. Two weeks ago we had Kermit and Miss Piggy and this week we had Oscar the Grouch from Sesame Street. We found out that Oscar isn't really all that grouchy because I made him laugh all the time he was here.

One of Mrs. Santa's biggest jobs up here at the North Pole is being in charge of the Surprise Shop, because it seems everyone wants surprises for Christmas. This is one of her favorite jobs because she can use her imagination and creativity.

Mrs. Santa is learning to knit and Terry, her instructor, started a big knitting circle called the Knittin' Needlers, with a bunch of the Brownies at the Heart of North Pole Medical Center. Every day someone new wants to join in the fun. Mrs. Santa didn't think she had the time, but after she saw one of the Brownies, Kat, finish a beautiful sweater, she just thought she wanted to learn to make one someday, too. Tammy B. is still working on her black sweater, but it's looking terrific, too.

Mrs. Santa and Coral are starting out making dish cloths because they are nice small projects. Coral thinks that's all she wants to make, but Terry will probably get her doing something big someday. Valerie knits a lot of scarves and you can be sure we need them up here at the North Pole! Tammy D. likes to see what everybody is making and is so busy she hardly has time to get to it. And we are all waiting for Elaine to get started; it looks like she will be next.

Colleen is in love with her grandchildren, so she is always knitting something neat for them. And the latest one to join the crowd is Heather. Mrs. Santa just could not believe it when she saw her knitting for the first time. She was really moving along quickly with her knitting needles. I think Daneen wanted to learn to knit, too, but she was too busy with her yoga. All I can say is that Terry started something big up here and I wonder if she knows what she got herself into!

What about the Brownies?

Now let me tell you about my Brownies. Children are always asking how many Brownies I have. The fact of the matter is that I really don't know because there are just too many to count. We get all of them together only two times during the year, and one of those times is for Thanksgiving dinner. Everyone looks forward to that. The dinner takes us one whole day because each of the Brownies has an opportunity to stand up and tell the rest of us just how thankful he or she is. Some of their stories are so heartwarming.

We usually have one other time when we try to get all the Brownies together. And that time is when we hold a birthday dinner for everyone. You see, we don't count birthdays up here. We think that is kind of silly. Age doesn't mean a thing to us. I don't even know how old Mrs. Santa is. So we just have one big birthday party for everyone, and the Brownies over in the Bake Shop have a really big blast baking for it.

Crusty, the chief baker, is the one who oversees this project and has been doing it for years. You can imagine how many Brownies it takes to make a cake that is big enough for all of the Brownies! That is quite a job.

One of the things I like most about my Brownies is the fact that they are always doing something for someone else. Just like Mrs. Santa, they, too, are so generous with their time. They will often go over to the Crippled Children's Hospital and read or play some kind of game with the little patients. They are always quick to help Mrs. Santa when they see she is overloaded with work. They constantly call her and ask if there is anything they can do to help her out.

Many of the Brownies also have little businesses, which they run when they are not busy working on our upcoming Christmas trip.

Sparky has his own Electrical Repair Shop, and Wigs has her own hair salon. Rocker has a music store called Rock with Me, and Woody has a furniture store. Close to my cabin is Sarah's Sweet Shop because Sarah, the owner, knows how much I like candy. She always keeps black licorice on her shelves because she knows that is a favorite of mine. I like the soft bite-sized pieces the best and she knows how to make them just right.

Austin runs the Healing Hands Animal Shelter and Spa. He takes in all kinds of animals, but he especially likes big dogs. He cares for the animals until they are in good health and then finds them a nice home or, if they are used to living in the wild, he takes them to the North Woods where they will be the happiest.

He uses special mineral waters for healing and gentle touch to help the animals trust him. He has a gift of knowing just how to treat each of the animals to bring them back to their best health. It is apparent to all of us up here that he has a very big heart.

During the winter months, Austin likes to snowboard up on Merry Mountain. He is amazing, but he is pretty daring. Mrs. Santa worries about him doing those tricks up there on the moguls.

Patti has her own clothing boutique called Classy Casuals and Puzzles. Doesn't that sound like a funny name for a shop?

Since Patti enjoys playing golf in the summer, she opened this store for other golfers who like to dress nicely. She is such a classy dresser herself and always looks so nice. She works out to keep herself in shape, and that helps her golf game. One of the things she likes to tease me about is her hole-in-one because she knows I got a hole-in-one pretty long ago. Her favorite golfing partner is Pope Peter, our highest ranking Brownie. The other Brownies respect him and like to see him at church on Sundays.

Patti also enjoys putting puzzles together, so she has a little section in her shop with boxes of puzzles stacked on top of each other. In the front of her shop, there is always a working puzzle on display, and her customers are welcome to tinker with it.

She has one puzzle in her house that is so big she has been working on it for three years. I think it's about time she brings that one to her shop so the customers can get busy and get it done! Her customers and her friends like Patti so much, not just because she is a fun person, but because she is also a very classy lassie!

Monica has a very unique shop, which is a combination nail salon and video store. She calls it Clips and Flicks. When she and her helpers are doing nails, they always have a movie playing. Sometimes the customers just stay for the whole movie, so she has a built-in theater room with lots of seating. Sometimes she has Murder She Wrote episodes or the Golden Girls playing, too. Monica's favorite Golden Girl is Sophia. She just loves her wisecracks. Of course, she provides popcorn and drinks too.

Customers often say the shop reminds them of a movie you have down there called Steel Magnolias. That's because all the customers know each other and they have the time of their lives catching up on each other's latest news. Monica is also a lawyer, but we don't have much of a need for that up here since everyone seems to be able to work out their differences. She is much happier in her shop because there is so much fun going on and lots of laughter.

She likes it when her husband, Elliot, surprises her by coming to the shop just to say "Hi." He is a very busy man because he is the program director for the Happy Hoopsters basketball team. He is great at keeping everything straight and he just loves his job!

Peggy is one of our most dependable Brownies. She really has her act together. Whenever the Brownies play their games, she is the team mother and always has her first-aid kit by her side. Peggy has always been one of those nurturing people who cares about and for others. She knows just what to do when someone gets hurt.

Because she is so organized, some of the other moms ask her for advice on keeping it all together. She just seems to "go with the flow." Sometimes Peggy likes to bake in her spare time, and she is really good at that. Mrs. Santa even gets recipes from her sometimes. Peggy has a bakeshop called Peggy's Delights and she definitely delights everyone who tries her goodies.

Sometimes she volunteers at the Children's Hospital and takes x-rays of the little ones. The doctors and the patients just love her because she always has a smile for them. You might be interested to know that Peggy and Patti are two of my original Brownies and have been with me for a very long time.

I'd like to tell you about one more of our Brownies, named Erin. She is now going to Icicle University and is working very hard. She loves all kinds of sports and is very athletic. She is also very good in math and writing, so she may end up running a sports training camp up here or writing about it. You have to know about finances if you want to have a successful business, so she is wise to study numbers.

I wonder if she will someday recruit softball players from down your way and bring them to the North Pole for training. I think she could help some of the players win more tournaments because she has a good head for the game.

Erin has played softball with the Fencebusters up here since she was little and is a great center fielder. Because she is a good leader, she has been the captain of the team. If she continues to keep up with her good work, I'm sure we'll be seeing her back here one day doing great things!

I must also tell you about Cassie, one of our oldest Brownies. She just turned 90 and is as alert as ever. Her nephew, Glendon, takes her to all the shows at the North Pole Music Theater and she just loves it. She also loves to watch those old Lawrence Welk shows because it brings back memories. She sometimes sings one of her favorite songs called "Barefoot Days." Cassie is a very kind person and we all just love her.

We also love our oldest Brownie, Pappy. He has a lot of experience, so the younger Brownies go to him for his wisdom.

Of course, we have our own doctor for the Brownies and his name is Dr. DooGood. He has his own Claus Clinic up here. Dr. Fillem is our dentist, but he doesn't have much work because our Brownies brush their teeth three times a day.

We have Brownie Boy Scouts and Brownie Girl Scouts up here too. The Brownie Girl Scouts sell snowballs, not cookies, and all of the money they collect is turned over to Santa's Healing Hospital. They don't want any money for themselves; they just want to make sure the money they collect can be put to the very best use to help others. This is typical of those of us up here at the North Pole. Whatever we can do for others, that is what we like to do.

Spic and Span are in charge of spring-cleaning at the Brownie cabins. Stamper serves as our postmaster and works a lot with our special delivery reindeer, Zip. Of course, Rackem, Packem and Stackem are in charge of loading the sleigh. They get their training in a sardine factory so they can really pack things tight! Tooter is our band director, and Strut is our drum majorette.

We have some twin Brownies up here and I'm sure you would like to know their names. Mike and Ike are not only twins, they work together as a team at the candy shop. Skittles is in charge of the candy shop and he is very happy with his workers because they all work together to make things easier for each other.

Pete and RePete are also twins and they work with Spokes over in the Car Shop. Wheels is the head of the shop, but Spokes is the Brownie manager who works the closest with the other Brownies. Wheels spends a lot of time doing the bookwork and making sure the overall operation is running smoothly.

Although I like to have a nice full beard, I do get it trimmed by our Brownie barber, Clipper. He has a couple of helpers and his first assistant barber is Whiskers. There are a couple of other Brownies in training right now because some of the older Brownies are in need of a trim and they don't have a lot of time to sit and wait. They would probably do well to get buzz cuts so they wouldn't have to get their hair cut so often. I don't think I would look too good in a buzz cut, do you?

For those of you who are interested in knowing what the Brownies do all year long, believe me, there is almost no limit to their activities. As you can well imagine, because of our climate up here, a lot of their activities focus on winter sports. They have their own Winter Olympics and some of the contests involve sled racing, ice skating, ice hockey, snowball throwing, snow skiing, and snowboarding.

For the sled racing, all of the Brownies are responsible for making their own sleds. Those races are held on Merry Mountain and the race is actually five miles long.

We have a huge ice skating pond that is indoors so they can ice skate all year round. We have one skater who is just phenomenal. He spins so fast that you can't tell his head from his feet. To top it off, he wrote his name in the ice with his skates. I never saw anyone do that before. His name is Spinner.

The Brownies also have lots of games they play all year long. For about six or seven months of the year, they have frequent snowball battles. They do have a rule, however, that you cannot hit anyone in the face. Sometimes Rudolph likes to get in the middle of those battles. Wherever there is any kind of a game going on, you can bet Rudolph and some of his reindeer are going to get involved.

Sometimes Rudolph brings the team down from the ranch and the Brownies each pick one of the reindeer to ride. They have snowball battles while they are riding on the backs of the reindeer. That's a real trick in itself.

One of their favorite games is Tug of Love. As I mentioned earlier, we don't have "Tug of War" up here, just Tug of Love. The winner of that game usually is on the receiving end of a cold dog and jumping bean supper prepared by the loser.

We don't give prizes, though, because we don't think everything needs a prize. We think it's nice to win, but we also believe winning is not everything. Doing the best you can is all we ever ask. We know that some of our Brownies work faster than others, and we know that some of the reindeer run faster than others; however, the important thing is always teamwork—working together—unselfishly to get the job done. It doesn't matter who gets the credit, and we don't believe in placing the blame on others.

The Brownies also have a lot of popcorn parties and taffy tugs as well as spelling bees, bake-offs, hoagie sales, sock hops and schools of all kinds. They have computer courses, carpentry schools, sewing classes and cooking classes. They have welding, drafting, nursing and decorating classes too.

Actually, they have anything that has to do with learning. They think learning is fun, and so do I. I learn many things from my Brownies, believe me. I even learn some things from Rudolph, as strange as that might sound.

Learning day after day is another important part of life at the North Pole. We believe that if you stop learning, you stop growing. We can never learn too much, and we learn lessons up here every day of our lives.

One great place to learn is at the huge library, which the Brownies built one summer. It has more than 250,000 books of all kinds, and many of the Brownies use some of their leisure time to go to the library and learn more about their favorite subjects. Our librarian, Pager, makes sure there are books in the library to fit everyone's interests.

The Brownies also run some of the shops in our malls and some of our restaurants too. We have several malls up here with a lot of different stores. We have the Frozen Mile Mall and the Claus Outlets. We also have the Polar Plaza.

We have so many different shops and stores that I couldn't possibly name them all. We have Brownies and Noble Bookstore, Pier Two, Chick-O's, Claus Carvers, the Polar Palace and many, many more.

We also have lots and lots of places to eat, as you might expect. With the way these Brownies work, they need to keep up their strength, so they eat a lot. Some of their favorite foods are polar pizza, snowball soup, polar popsicles, macaroni and cheesesicles, roasted snowflake sandwiches, and grilled icicle burgers.

Some of their favorite restaurants are McSanta's, Windy's, Snowburger King, and Freeze and Frizzy. They also like to eat at Barbie's Bar-B-Q, Rudolph's Rib Palace, Frozen Fries, Long John Shivers, The Ice Palace, The Igloo, the Polar Pancake House, Polar Pizza Shack, U-Hop, Wimpy's, and of course, my favorite, Santa's Steakhouse. It makes my mouth water just to say that!

One of the other things my Brownies enjoy doing very much is having a prayer circle. Anytime they hear that someone is struggling with a problem, illness or sickness, they put their names in the prayer circle. Believe me, that is a lot of power, when all of my Brownies and Mrs. Santa and I are in one big prayer circle. We know where to look when we or someone else needs help.

A very important part of life at the North Pole is having enough churches to take care of all of our Brownies and our friends. We have churches for all denominations. Just to name a few, we have St. Christopher's, St. Santa's, St. Nick's, the Tall Timber Tabernacle, and our largest church, LKEC. Those letters mean Love Keeps Everyone Close.

One of the things we like best about that church is that it welcomes everyone no matter what and tries to bring everyone together by showing love. All of us have a part to play in the church of our choosing. Each church has its own choir and its own service. The Brownies always have an annual candlelight service on Christmas Eve and it is so beautiful and touching.

What do Rudolph and his team do the rest of the year?

Another subject children want to know more about is Rudolph and his team. Well, there is plenty to say about this group. Rudolph is definitely the leader, but there is more than one reindeer team. One is the regular group that most of you are familiar with, but Rudolph has two backup teams. After all, we need to make sure that if something happens to one of the reindeer we will be ready with a backup.

One year we did have a little incident when Comet came down with the hoofing cough. We didn't panic because we knew we had Ajax standing by to move into Comet's place.

If Rudolph needs backup, he can count on his wife, Pinky, to stand in for him. He brought her along once or twice to make sure she got to know all of the ins and outs of the trip and how to use all the magic moves he has been using for years. Other backup reindeer include Tapper for Dancer, Preppy for Prancer, Deener, who is Donner's wife, for him, Blaster for Blitzen, Siren for Vixen, Arrow for Cupid, and Dipper for Dasher.

You might wonder what the reindeer do all year round. Well, I can tell you this. They do not have much time to rest because Rudolph knows how important it is to keep them in tip-top shape.

He has training schools of all kinds for them. He has a flight school, a direction school and also a fitness-training program that is second to none. They practice six hours a day all year round. You may think that is a lot of work, but for them it is more like play than work.

The reindeer live on the Reindeer Ranch and they always have activities going on there. They have reindeer rides, reindeer races, reindeer Olympics, a reindeer obstacle course and their own reindeer roundups. They also have animal clinics, where they train other animals up here in the North Woods.

Once a month Rudolph has a reindeer ramble up at the Reindeer Ranch, and they do a lot of square dancing and line dancing. If you want to see something funny, you should see the reindeer line dancing. The clacking and hoof-stomping really make a racket. They sure know how to "hoof it up!" They even do the antler shake with bells on their antlers. Just this year, Rudolph added a new group of dancers called the Reindeer Rockettes. When they are all lined up in a row and they kick their legs high, it is something to see!

Rudolph has trained some of the reindeer to run snow blowers to make sure all of the sidewalks up here between the cabins are kept free of snow. You can imagine that keeps a lot of them busy. We have a few reindeer that do special delivery work and Zip is in charge of that.

And, as I mentioned in some of my previous letters, I am so proud of the reindeer who go over to the Crippled Children's Hospital and take the children for rides. The children just love that. The reindeer also take the older people who can't get out on their own to different places on their sleds. The staff at the hospital put some of the them on a big sled and then Rudolph and the reindeer take them to their favorite restaurants. That is a big thing up here for people who cannot get out on their own.

As you can imagine, Rudolph is very sensitive to all of the other animals up here at the North Pole. He was named "Animal of the Year" 10 out of the last 12 years. The other two times they wanted to give it to him, but he felt that his friend, Smokey the Bear, deserved the award because he knows that Smokey the Bear does a lot of great things.

We do not allow hunting of any kind up here in the North Woods. I have my own organization called the S.P.A.A., which stands for Santa Protects All Animals. Every now and then, on one of his trips to the North Woods for fireplace wood, Rudolph will find animals that have been hurt. He will always bring them in and make sure they get the best of care. Sometimes the animals are so weak because they can't find food, and sometimes the weather is just too cold for them. Rudolph always brings those animals to the North Pole vet to get checked out.

Our vet's name is Dr. DooMuch. We don't have any Dr. DooLittle's up here because that wouldn't work too well. There isn't anything Dr. DooMuch doesn't know about animals. Obviously, there are times when the reindeer come down with something like the hoofing cough or the reindeer rash, or even hoof and mouth disease, so we have to be prepared for everything.

Rudolph has some of his own pet foods that he likes to bring along on the big trip. It doesn't matter what kind of animal it is, he always has some kind of pet food available. He has his own supply store up here and he calls it Rudolph's Rations.

Some of the animals' favorite foods are Kitten Kurls, Polar Pellets, and Hush Puppies. You do know, don't you, that Hush Puppies keep the dogs from barking when we come around on the trip? Rudolph also has Reindeer Rigatoni, Frosted Spaghettios, Marshmallow Melons, and Pea-na-beans. That is a cross between peas and beans.

Sometimes children ask what Rudolph's favorite foods are and I would have to say hay, carrots, apples, and believe it or not, ice cream. He loves peanut butter, too, but it always seems to get stuck to the roof of his mouth.

Where Do You Go on Vacation?

Children often ask if Mrs. Santa and I take vacations. We sure do! One of our most enjoyable places to visit is Williamsburg, Virginia. We like to spend a week there almost every year.

We have our favorite restaurants that we always go to for dinner. One of them is named the Fat Canary, which we think is a very interesting name. After a few dinners there, we learned to know a gentleman by the name of Tom Power who, along with his wife Mary Ellen, and their children, Cathy, Mary Ellen and Tom Jr., opened this wonderful restaurant, as well as The Cheese Shop adjoining it.

When we came back from one of our Williamsburg vacations, I could not wait to tell the Brownies all about our visit to the Fat Canary. So, at the next Brownie meeting, I made sure it was on the agenda. After hearing about it, the Brownies decided to take the idea to the Brownie Better Business Bureau and propose opening a few new restaurants up here at the North Pole.

Instead of the Fat Canary, they suggested opening The Plump Penguin. They would like to have the servers sing Happy Dancing whenever someone dining there has a birthday. We are already thinking of having Tom-Tom be the chef.

Since our other favorites are the art café 26, Le Yaca, and La Petite Tea Room, the Brownies are working on some great ideas revolving around those restaurants, too. They are focusing on superb customer care because they know how important that is. We may have some of the Brownies visit Sibilla, Daniele and Jean to experience the exceptional hospitality they share with their restaurateurs.

What does the North Pole look like?

In order to give you a picture of what our community looks like up here, I thought I would just tell you the names of some of the streets. There is Pleasant Street, Smile Alley, Brownie Boulevard and Reindeer Ranch Road. We also have Bell Boulevard, Santa Street, Snowflake Circle, Lively Lane and Love Lane.

We have some neat names up here, don't we? If you will notice, they are happy names. Some others are Noel Court, Hug Alley, Carol Lane, Whisker Lane, Deer Boulevard, Kozy Street, Marshmallow Lane, Blizzard Boulevard and Icicle Avenue.

Believe me, it is not all work and no play up here. We believe you should work hard but we also believe you should have time to play, too. The Brownies have all kinds of sports teams up here. As I mentioned earlier, their basketball team is called The Happy Hoopsters and they are so fast.

The football team is called the Brownie Bombers. Their quarterback is named Bullseye, and Toejammer is the kicker. Both of them are terrific and play in the Super Saucer every year. We don't have a Super Bowl up here—we have a Super Saucer. Their biggest opponents are the South Polecats but they usually don't have too much trouble with them. As a matter of fact, nine out of the last 10 times they skunked them.

The baseball team is called Santa's Sluggers and their pitcher's name is Blur. He throws the ball so fast that the batters usually can't see it. They also have a softball team called the Fencebusters. Boy, can they hit the ball!

We have a new softball team up here this year called the Heartbreakers and their star slugger is Erin. She is one powerhouse! Their coach, Terry, has been around for a long time and so many of our opponents end up frustrated because our games are just heartbreakers for them when they lose. Terry's wife, Barbara, comes to all of the games, and they are quite a team. Next to Erin's grandpa, Barbara is one of their biggest fans.

The Brownies even have a bowling team called the Alley Cats. They also have a soccer team called the Brownie Booters. Their goalie's name is Stretch, and it is almost impossible to get one by him.

We have a Brownie band called the Notebusters and they play at every one of the Brownie sporting events. Mrs. Santa's cheerleaders, the Snowbelles, are also present at every sporting event. They certainly do know how to make a lot of noise. I think their cheering helps the Brownies win so many of their games.

We have a couple of movie theaters up here. One is called the Cinnamon Cinema, and we also have a TV station, W.O.W. This is where I have my TV program called Santa's Showcase.

There is never a dull moment up here at the North Pole. We even have a suggestion box on the outside of my cabin in case any of the Brownies has a suggestion for a new activity. Every day, we check the box to see if there is a good idea that we should be carrying out. We have sweetheart dances on Valentine's Day, and we celebrate Easter with a snowball roll instead of an egg roll. We have more snowballs than we have eggs.

This gives you a good idea of what goes on up here all year round at the North Pole. Obviously our biggest thrill is on Christmas Eve when the sleds are packed, the shelves are empty and we are off on the big trip. There's nothing more exciting than when we lift off in my Dream Sleigh Christmas Eve.

Our trips are usually very smooth, and we rarely run into any problems. We did have a couple of close shaves with a few comets and meteors, but we always came through without a scratch. We stay on Cloud Nine as long as possible and then hop onto the Milky Way. We have our own special ray of light to take us where we want to go and, of course, Rudolph's red nose follows it and brightens up everything.

After the big trip when we land back at the North Pole, we are always delighted to be part of the Welcome Back Party. That is a celebration to see! Last year, there were 101 floats with each one holding a sleek looking Dalmatian. Ninety-two bands came from all over the world.

The South Pole always has a great marching band called the Stepups. Rudolph is as proud as can be as he wears his favorite red blanket on his back and silver bells around his neck. He stands so tall!

I hope you have been able to sit back and enjoy reading about our fantasyland at the North Pole. I think we should always keep that little child within us close, and perhaps I have helped you release the little child within you.

Yes, imagination is what keeps my letter writing alive - not just my imagination but the children's as well. As you will be able to see in these letters from John, he has no lack of imagination. However, to John, this is real. I just fell in love with his letters from 2007.

John was thoughtful enough to write three letters, one to Santa, one to Mrs. Santa, and one to The Elves. That, in itself, is very unusual. They were certainly some of the most creative letters I have received in the more than 100,000, which I have answered over the years. The context of these letters knocked my socks off! And that's not easy to do after all these years.

John really rocks, just as he said, "You rock," to Mrs. Santa in his letter to her. Of course Mrs. Santa rocks. We both rock because we got each other rocking chairs last year. Ho! Ho!

> *"Dear the Elves,*
> *My name is John. I appreciate how much work you put into making everyones Christmas special. I've always wanted to see the elf village. It must be so much fun working for Santa and Mrs. Claus!*
>
> *Are any of you interested in coming to live with me? If not tell your friends or relatves that I am looking for an elf to live with me. If you don't want to be seen by anone other than my family, I would not tell anybody about you.*

You would also be given a seat at mealtimes, given your own room, and have your run of the house.

Your favorite foods will be cooked. I am nine years old. A baby elf would probably suit, but if it is an older elf that would be good, too. If y ou would like to live at my house, mail a letter to me.

Best wishes for Christmas and the New Year,
Your Friend, John"

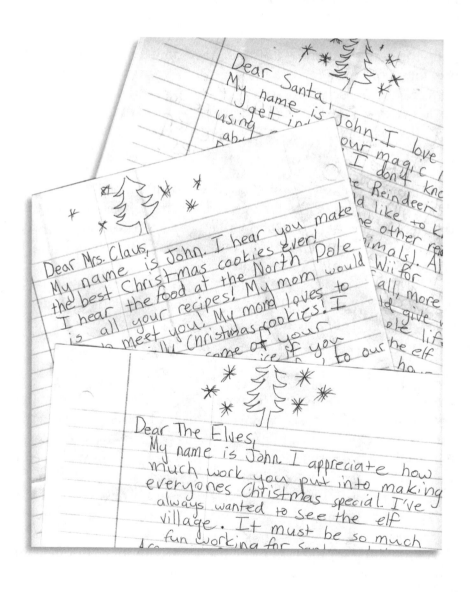

At times, I receive a letter to Santa when it is too close to Christmas to get the letter back to the child in time. I am very sensitive to the hearts of my little friends, so I have to be very careful when I answer these letters.

If I am not sure whether or not the letter will make it to the child in time, I might write something like this. "I don't know when you wrote your letter, but I just got it today and it is the first day of winter, December 21. I think the postman must have gotten lost on his way to our post office. I sure hope my answer gets to you before I do. But remember, the important thing is that I got your letter before we started loading our sleigh, Santa's Dream Sled. I made sure I hit the hotline button to alert the Brownies."

If I am certain the letter will not arrive in time for Christmas, I handle it a different way. I will hold the letter until after Christmas and then write a different type of letter. I will let my imagination run wild with stories about "the trip."

I might say, "By this time, you know I did not have time to write to you before my big trip. I sure hope I did okay for you, though. Next year you'll have to write a little earlier. If you were not pleased with your presents, you could write another letter to me and I will do better the next time." Of course, the thrill of Christmas and opening the presents is still fresh in their minds, so I have never gotten a second letter expressing displeasure from a child.

I continue with highlights about our big trip on Christmas Eve. "We had a beautiful trip to your house and Rudolph and the team made absolutely no mistakes. I took a picture of your decorations so I could show them to Mrs. Santa. Since she can't come along on the trip, she likes it when I bring back pictures. I always have the Brownie camera with me on the trip.

Mrs. Santa is busy arranging our Welcome Home Party and Parade while we are out delivering presents. Well, she sure did have a big party for us when we got back. She outdoes herself every year. She and the others are always so happy when we return safely.

This year, Rudolph used Cloud Nine a lot on our trip. It was a very smooth trip. Rudolph was so proud of his whole team again this year. We didn't have to make any sudden stops and we stayed right on schedule. Since the postman slows down sometimes because he gets tired as Christmas approaches, please try to send your letter earlier next year and then you will be sure to get an answer before Christmas." I'm sure you noticed that I always ask them to write earlier next year. I just have to hope Mommy or Daddy gets the hint!

The most frustrating thing for me is to receive a letter without a complete address. There is no way for me to respond to this child who is anxiously awaiting his or her letter, and it just breaks my heart to know of their disappointment.

suspect that my imagination grows and stretches every time I answer children's letters. I know I had to stretch my mind to come up with an answer to this next letter, which showed some imagination itself! I will let you read his entire letter because it is one of a kind.

"Dear Santa,
My grammy is writing this letter for me. You see, I wasn't born yet. My birthday should be in late April. Mommy and Daddy love me so very, very much. Mommy had a slight problem and had to have more testing done. They found out I am a boy! Everyone is very happy. My name will be Mason. Next year I will write again but all my grammy wants for Christmas is for me to be a healthy, happy baby. Maybe you could send me a return letter. My mommy and my grammy both wrote to you as a child. When I arrive, I will have to get used to my first real pet. He is a Yorkie named Maverick. We will have a lot of fun together. Mommy already said Daddy will have a Sony PlayStation buddy. My family loves me so much already. Please say a prayer so that my grammy gets her Christmas wish of one healthy grandson. Thanks so much for listening. Your unborn friend, Mason."

As you can tell, his Grammy wrote this letter. It isn't unusual for this to happen since I am in my third generation of writing letters and a lot of the grandparents are now writing for their grandchildren. This letter was a little unique in that the child was not even born yet! I must admit this was a "first" for Santa Claus.

When I answered Mason's letter, among many other things, I did say that when I told Mrs. Santa his name was going to be Mason that really made her smile. She said, "Oh, I really like the name, Mason. As a matter of fact, my favorite canning jars are called Mason." I'm sure Grammy had a big laugh over this. Now I receive letters from Mason himself and Grandma can take a break.

Chapter Six

Santa Wraps Presents with Loving Care

We all have so much to give and so much to learn. My mother used to say, "Learn to listen and listen to learn." That was such good advice. She also used to say, "Keep your mind open and something might drop in." I never thought of my mother as being much of a philosopher, but she did have a lot of common sense.

Another piece of advice that has stayed with me is a verse, which I first read about 50 years ago and which I have recited to audiences all over the country. The words in this verse have helped me tremendously when dealing with my own difficulties and challenges in life regarding my health.

If I knew the author, I certainly would give him or her credit; however, I have always seen "Author Unknown" following these beautiful words.

"The World Is Mine"

Today upon a bus I saw a girl with golden hair.
She seemed so gay I envied her and wished that I were half so fair.
I watched her as she rose to leave and saw her hobble down the aisle;
She had one leg and wore a crutch, but as she passed — a smile.
Oh, God, forgive me when I whine; I have two legs and the world is mine.

Later on I bought some sweets. The boy who sold them had such charm,
I thought I'd stop and talk awhile. If I were late, 'twould do no harm.
And as we talked he said, "Thank you sir. You've really been so kind.
It's nice to talk to folks like you because you see, I'm blind."
Oh, God, forgive me when I whine; I have two eyes and the world is mine.

Later walking down the street I met a boy with eyes so blue;
But he stood and watched the others play — it seemed he knew not what to do.
I paused, and then I said, "Why don't you join the others, dear?"
But he looked straight ahead without a word, and then I knew, he couldn't hear.
Oh, God, forgive me when I whine; I have two ears and the world is mine.

Two legs to take me where I go;
Two eyes to see the sunset's glow;
Two ears to hear all that I should know.
Oh, God, forgive me when I whine; I'm blest indeed — for this world is mine.

I think this verse would be good to pass along to anyone you may know who is frustrated because he or she is dealing with problems. We all need to be reminded to appreciate the blessings we have and make our world better by opening our hearts to others.

There are so many opportunities for us to touch the lives of others in special ways. A word of kindness, a bit of encouragement, and true listening to those who simply need an audience of one go a long way in lifting people up. I am very careful about how I answer children's letters because I want them to know I really "listen" when I read them.

Children place their trust in Santa because they know he is listening very carefully to their every word. If we want our children to listen to us, we would do well by setting the example of being a good listener to them, too. One of the greatest compliments one can give is to listen, truly listen.

My answers to the children are wrapped with words of loving care. Words of praise and stickers are my way of encouraging the child who wrote the letter.

I love to get personal with the children and I can do that with the parents' help. I often tell the parents to make sure they put in their own little note to give me the benefit of knowing some facts about their children.

If I know the names of their pets and the names of their playmates, I can be very personal. If I know the name of their school and their teacher's name, or any specific interests such as sports enjoyed and favorite teams, I can be even more brilliant! When I know their families, I can even talk to the children about their dad and mom on very personal terms. No two letters are alike.

Keep in mind that I answer all the questions children ask. Many children have the same questions. All of them want to know whether Santa comes into the house through the chimney and what happens if they don't have one. They all seem to be curious about how I can get to all the houses in one night, too. They also want to know how the reindeer fly. Of course, I have explanations for all these questions and I try to be as realistic as possible.

I am not going to tell children that my reindeer can fly because you must have wings to fly, and they know that reindeer do not have wings. So, I explain to them that the reindeer have "magic movements" and it almost looks like they can fly. Obviously, up at the North Pole, we have a lot of things that involve magic.

I don't tell them I'm coming down their chimneys. Not every house has a chimney—so if children do not have a chimney on their house, they may come to the conclusion that Santa can't come to their house. I tell them the chimneys are getting smaller and my insurance rates are going up. And Mrs. Santa doesn't like it when I come home with a sooty suit. I just tell them I have a master key that opens every door, so I will probably use the back door because that is usually closest to the kitchen. And I do know that my snack is usually on the kitchen table, so that is quite convenient.

We at the North Pole like to be role models for the children and give them positive reinforcement. I enjoy praising children and will often send them special awards such as a shiny red heart sticker called the "Glittering Heart Award," the "Way to Go Award" or the "Snowflake Award." If they have misbehaved, I try to convince them to change their ways. Children who need a special nudge in the right direction get stickers of bees that tell them to "Bee Polite" or "Bee Honest." The following letters are just a couple of examples.

"Hi Kaitlyn and Emily,
WOW! The first thing I must say is how excited we all were up here when we found out you were potty-trained by Emily, Kaitlyn. She must be a really good big sister. Kaitlyn, we know Emily helped you, but we also know that you must have tried really hard. When I told Mrs. Santa, she was so proud of you and said I must send you a special 'WAY TO GO' award. She told all the Brownies and they clapped and cheered and said, 'Oh, yes, we must send Kaitlyn a special award.'

Emily, it was hard for us to believe that you were able to potty-train Kaitlyn already. And it is neat that Kaitlyn is not having many accidents. I know that must make mom and dad REALLY happy.

It certainly won't be hard to please you this year. I know Kaitlyn does not know a lot about me yet, but I know you will explain me to her, Emily. You are such a good big sister."

When children misbehave, I don't look at them as being bad because we know all of us have imperfections. However, some children will hear about it from Santa if they haven't been on their best behavior. For instance, I ran into an acquaintance who told me her granddaughter was writing on walls with a crayon. I wrote the little girl a letter that said,

"Rudolph and I do check-up trips. On one of those trips we turned at that little street beside your house. And while we were sitting in the sleigh we could see right in your window and we saw some little girl writing on the wall with crayons. We're not sure who it was but we're sure it wasn't you. We can't have that, you know. I didn't like that very much and I had to make a note of it."

The next time the grandmother saw me, she reported that her granddaughter had stopped writing on the walls! So, I'm saying that if Santa can get through when others can't, so be it.

Children also frequently ask about Mrs. Santa and the elves. We prefer to call the elves Brownies up here at the North Pole. Everyone loves Brownies. We have as many girl Brownies as boy Brownies because, after all, we have equal opportunity for everyone.

If children tell me they are having a birthday, I make sure I include one of my "Happy Birthday" stickers with my letter. I tell them we all got together and sang a big "Happy Birthday" for them and ate some birthday cake to remember them.

I have stickers for any imaginable activity or sport. I also have an ample supply of stickers of pets. If they talk about their cat, then I send them a picture of one of our cats up here at the North Pole. If they have a dog for a pet, I send them a sticker of one of our dogs. They can't possibly have anything that I don't have up here.

If they talk about soccer, I talk about my soccer team. If they talk about football, I'm a football fan. If they want a certain numbered jersey, I will know which player's jersey they are asking for and I will mention the name of that particular player in my answer to them. At times, I will even send them a football or baseball card along with their letter. As you can see, I give each letter my personal attention.

I also like to personalize my responses by inserting some true facts about my life along with the fantasy. You see, I used to play the saxophone and Mrs. Santa really can't sing very well. That is true, as I told this little guy, Travis.

"Hi Travis,
I couldn't believe it when I heard you want a saxophone. I wonder if you knew that I play the saxophone? Mrs. Santa loves to hear me play it. She sings along when I play. One of our favorite songs is 'Santa Claus is Coming to Town.' I bet your mommy would sing that song to you right now if you asked her. Hopefully she sings better than Mrs. Santa. I always tell Mrs. Santa she sounds good, but the truth is that she doesn't sing all that well.

Since I know you like hockey and football, Travis, I thought I would send you a picture of one of the footballs and hockey sticks we use up here. Did you know we have an ice hockey team up here? They are called the Brownie Slapsticks. You should see them play. They scoot through each other's legs sometimes and it is hard to keep track of them.

I know you have a dog named Toby and I thought you would like to see one of our dogs up here. We have a lot of animals up here, but the dogs are usually the ones that hang around my cabin the most. This one is named Hobie. Isn't he a cute one? Hey, did you know that Hobie rhymes with Toby? Toby—Hobie—Hear it? I can't believe Toby likes marshmallows. I tried to feed them to Hobie and he just kept chewing and chewing and chewing. I don't think he liked the way they felt in his teeth. But the Brownies love them. They especially love to toast marshmallows over the campfire.

Well, I can't wait to see what you leave me for a snack on Christmas Eve. Rudolph asked me to remind you that he likes snacks, too. He likes carrots and apples the best. Sometimes he likes ice cream for a change. If you decide to leave some ice cream and it is melted in the bowl, Rudolph

*will just drink it. He likes it that way too. Well I'll be
seeing you Christmas Eve. Bye now.
Love, Santa."*

Some of the most enjoyable letters for me to answer are those to children whose
parents or grandparents I know very well. I will often use a lot of humor aimed at
the parent or grandparent because I know they will read the letter, too. As a matter
of fact, I am often told they enjoy the letters as much as the child!

For me, there is nothing sweeter than to be able to be Santa Claus to my very own
granddaughter. Of course, I must tell you about some of my answers to my real-life
granddaughter, Erin, living in McSherrystown, Pennsylvania. I thought I would
extract some paragraphs from various letters, which will let you know how I used
my very close knowledge about her life to make her letters more believable. Her
father, Chuck, and her mother, Peg, helped keep me informed. It was so much fun to
refer to "Grandpa" in her letters, since I am both Grandpa and Santa Claus to her.

*"Dear Erin,
Your grandpa sent me your letter and asked me if I could
answer it right away. He and I are good friends and he
told me you are the latest love in his life and the best thing
that's happened to him in a long time.*

*I know you are only four and you can't write your own
letter, but it did sound like you were telling Mommy what
to say. I didn't know your mommy was 37. Wow! She looks
like she is only 27! She must be eating a lot of carrots and
celery. That keeps a person young. And Rudolph, too. He
eats that stuff all the time and look how fast he can run!
He has better knees than your mommy, though."*

made this reference because Erin's mother had to have surgery on one of her knees.

*"Thank you for the coloring you sent me. I have it up on
the Brownie refrigerator so everyone can see it. If I want
someone to see something, I put it on the refrigerator. I*

saw your refrigerator one time and it had a picture of Mommy and Aunt Patti and Grandpa on it. Your grandpa's whiskers are the same color as mine but they aren't as long as mine.

I know you have been going to bed without crying and that makes me very happy. When you don't like something, don't you put that little lower lip out? If it gets too low, you might step on it!

I hear you are going to Mrs. Day's School now and you are learning to do a lot of neat things. I know most of your friends in your class. If you get your picture taken again this year, will you leave one by your snack for me to bring back to show Mrs. Santa? I'm always talking about how cute you are.

I know you went to see my old friend, Mickey Mouse, down at Disney World. Did you know he is as old as your grandpa? Did you get caught in the rain down there and wear one of those yellow Mickey raincoats? Aren't they fun?

Now, Erin, I heard that you get some 'hissy-fits' sometimes and then you cry and stomp your feet. None of us like that and I know it makes Mommy and Daddy sad."

I guess you can see how I'm trying to help out Erin's mother and father here, can't you?

"I don't want you to be like that Oscar the Grouch. He called me on my telephone, and do you know what he said to me? He said, 'Have a rotten day' and I told him to fall into a mud puddle.

Gracious me, I found out you are going to be in a wedding. I guess you will carry the ring and wear flowers in your hair. I must say you are really the cutest little girl on all my stops, and I like to see your smile. I want you to give lots of smiles away. I would like to see a picture of you when you are dressed for the wedding. Maybe you could send me one.

Your house is always decorated so nicely. That mother of

yours is quite a decorator, isn't she? You know, I might have to bring Daddy a gun that shoots a little straighter this year. You tell your dad not to bring his gun up here because we don't allow any hunting in the North Woods. Speaking of Daddy, I think he must have put up that big swing set in your yard that Rudolph and I saw on one of our check-up trips.

When I told Mrs. Santa you were going to have cheese and crackers and Sarsaparilla for me, she wanted to come along. She knows I never get Sarsaparilla anywhere else. I told her it was much better than snowball juice."

You can see by this next letter that as Erin got older, I could talk to her in a more grown-up way.

"Erin, it sounds like you are really into football. Wow, you know the good ones—Steve Young and Jerry Rice. Our Brownies like the 49ers, too. Steve Young is a nifty left-hander, and you know those left-handers are something else!"

I thought you might like to know that Erin is left-handed, so this line was especially for her.

"Don't you worry—we won't let your golden retriever, Bailey, out of the foyer. Rudolph said he thinks he will bring Bailey some of his reindeer food to see if he likes it. Rudolph said Bailey is almost big enough to be on his reindeer team!

Do you think Aunt Patti and Uncle Pete will come for Christmas dinner? I know Aunt Patti comes to your house to eat sometimes. She likes pork chops and red licorice. Oh, did you and Aunt Patti go 'power shopping' lately? She really knows how to find the bargains. She did buy Uncle Pete some golf balls one time that went crooked, though.

And yes, I know Allison's house is in Maryland and I know exactly which one it is. I know what she wants from me for Christmas, too. She is getting to be such a pretty girl. I think I'll bring her a sweatshirt from Michigan.

It is time for me to go to choir practice. I'm singing a solo in church Sunday. I hope the same thing doesn't happen to me again this time. I hit a note so low they had to get two Brownies to help it up. Mrs. Santa started to laugh and got the hiccups, so we had to put peanut butter on the roof of her mouth to stop the hiccups. She got to like peanut butter so now I make her peanut butter fudge all the time.

Well, Erin, I'll be seeing you soon in McSherrystown, Pennsylvania. I'm sending you some hugs and kisses. Bye now. Love, Santa."

At this writing, Erin is in her freshman year at Iona College in New Rochelle, New York, and was awarded academic and athletic scholarships.

As you can see, I ended Erin's letter the way I often end letters, with some kind of reason why I must wrap it up. Sometimes it's Mrs. Santa calling me for supper or perhaps it is Rudolph asking me to come to the Reindeer Ranch to see their latest drill.

It could be that my red hotline button lights up and Mrs. Santa is frantic because the wig machine went berserk again in the Doll Workshop. Of course, it just could be that Zip, my special delivery reindeer, has just come into my cabin with hoofsful of letters from my little friends.

Friendship with children and adults alike is very important to me, and we are fortunate to have a family we hold close in our group of "true friends." John and Lynn Boyer, from Lancaster, Pennsylvania, have been two of our most caring friends, and their daughters, Jayne and Whitney, are held just as close in our hearts. I have watched these "little girls" grow up to be two fine young ladies with good values and morals, which were demonstrated by their parents. You can feel the closeness by reading this letter from Santa.

"Hi Jayne and Whitney,
Do you know what I am doing as I write this letter to you?
I called Mrs. Santa over to my cabin and we are listening to the Christmas carols you sent me. What a nice sound! I know we will listen to them in the next few weeks. Thank you.

I was trying to think of the things you like. I know you like basketball cards, Jayne, because you are so good at playing basketball. David Robinson is probably your favorite. And Whitney, I know you like to collect perfume bottles. Am I right? One night when you were sleeping I looked into your bedroom and I saw those little dolls for every year. That is a nice collection. Jayne, I am sending you one of my basketball cards. Take good care of it because it is a good card. Whitney, I can't send you any perfume bottles in this envelope, but I'll be remembering you.

I'm glad you left the gift choices up to me because I like picking things for you. Of course, I let Mrs. Santa give me some good ideas, too. When I told her about your basketball playing skills, Jayne, she said she wished you could play for our girl Brownie basketball team, the Happy Hens, up here. I know your daddy was captain of the basketball team at Franklin and Marshall College. He probably taught you a few new moves.

I'll bet you had fun in New York City. That Christmas show is SANTASTIC! It sounds like you've been doing lots of traveling. WOW! Sea World and Disneyland. Atlanta sounds like fun, too.

I can't wait to see your house. Your mommy does make it look like a dream world. She is so good at decorating. Maybe she won't have time to make any cookies this year. That's okay. I really don't need any snacks. Mrs. Santa is going to weigh me again this year before I leave for my trip and then she will weigh me when I get back to see how much I gained from eating all those snacks. She is something.

I hope Molly is behaving herself. Rudolph wanted me to ask about her. I thought you might like to see another picture of one of my dogs. His name is Fringes. He is so playful. Yesterday he got a hold of one of Mrs. Santa's balls of yarn and he had it all over the place! He looked like he was trying to wrap up the whole house as a package.

*I know it is not fair to pick favorites of all the little friends
I visit, but I just can't help it. The two of you are some of
my very favorites and I think some of that is because your
Mommy and Daddy have always been two of my favorites.
If you grow up to be like them, I will be so proud of you.*

*Well, I have lots more letters to write so I'll have to say,
'So long' for now. I'll remember to say a special prayer for
your family tonight when Mrs. Santa and I say our prayers
together. Bye now.*
Love, Santa."

Now let me update you on Jayne and Whitney. After graduating from the University
of Delaware, Jayne joined Athletes in Action, a ministry of Campus Crusade for
Christ. She will be marrying Kyle, who is also a part of this ministry, and they will
be working together in North Carolina. Whitney works full time at an accounting
firm. She also enjoys her love of fashion working part time at Ann Taylor LOFT.

Another family we stay close to is Mrs. Santa's nephew, Kevin, and his wife, Mika,
from Bernville, Pennsylvania. They have two little ones who love writing to Santa, and
I just love writing back to them. I know a lot about them, so I can be very personal.

"Hi Cole and Kyra,
*Well, you sent me two prize-winning letters again this year.
Cole, your handwriting is just SANTASTIC! Kyra, since you
are only in the first grade, it is hard to believe that you could
print so well. I don't know if you had help, but either way,
it was TERRIFIC! I asked Liner, my best Brownie printer
what he thought of your letter and he said you need a 'WOW'
award. I guess you know that 'WOW' spelled backwards is
still 'WOW.'*

*Cole, you really made Rudolph extra happy when you drew
a picture of him. He wanted to know if he could put it up on
the reindeer bulletin board at the reindeer ranch. As you know,*

it's hard to keep any kind of a secret from me, and I heard that you read the Christmas Story with your dad at a Christmas breakfast. I understand everyone clapped for you, too.

Since you play football and baseball, Cole, I thought you might be interested in a couple of my old cards. As you might guess, most of my cards are very old ones. I am sending you Ricky Proehl and he is still playing; I know that. Here's one of Bobby Thompson, too. I'll bet your dad will know both of them.

It was thoughtful of you to say you won't be upset if you don't get everything on your list. That means you understand that I have many, many stops, and in some cases, some of the little boys and girls don't have much. Since you are such a caring little guy, I can see why you would say that.

Kyra, I hope this letter gets to you on the 21st of December because I know it is your birthday and this would be a nice birthday present. The Brownies will be singing 'Happy Birthday to You.' Crummy, one of my Brownie bakers is sending you a picture of a cake he is making up here. We will have to eat it up here because it's a little too late to send it to your house. By the way, Mrs. Santa told me they had a contest and they voted you the 'Best Dressed Girl' on our list. She said there wasn't anyone even close. One of my Brownies told me you got a new doll recently. I'm not sure about the name, but I think it might have been Mika, like your mother.

I guess you are still doing ballet aren't you? That will keep you 'on your toes.' I'll bet you have the prettiest tutu in your class. I see that you asked for a hula hoop, Kyra. That makes me laugh because I used to see Mrs. Santa try to make her hula hoop stay up on her hips. She said it was good exercise. I'll bet your mother would be good at that. I think that would make me dizzy.

Cole and Kyra, not too many children are getting perfect marks in school, but it doesn't surprise me that you are.

Mrs. Kowzlowski and Miss Kramer must be happy having the two of you as students. Keep up the good work.

Kyra, I am sorry your hamster, Fuzzy, went up to Hamster Heaven, but you will probably get a new one and maybe you will call that one Wuzzy. Cole, I'll bet Aldo is glad he found a happy home. We don't have many turtles up here. I think it's because the weather is too cold and they would have trouble walking on the ice. They don't go very fast anyhow.

Well, this letter got to be a long one, but I really like getting your letters and answering them. Happy Birthday, Kyra. See you both on Christmas Eve.
Love, Santa."

Andrew, another one of Mrs. Santa's nephews, has had some challenges lately as he puts great effort into recovering from a severe car accident. It was a nice surprise when I got a letter to Santa from him recently. You see, even those in their twenties can use a lift from Santa Claus sometimes. I tried keeping things light in my answer to him by having fun and, at the same time, letting him know how much I appreciate his positive attitude.

"Hi Andrew,
HO! HO! HO! What a nice surprise to hear from you. I'm sorry it took so long for me to get back to you, but Mrs. Santa and I were on a little vacation and are still trying to get caught up. We were all so glad to hear how much you liked your Christmas presents. We sure were hoping you would like your new radio and amplifier. The Brownies worked hard on that and it took a bunch of them working together to pull it off. We knew your dad would be good with the wiring part and were pretty sure he would get 'charged up' with that project. Our chief electrician, Sparky, was anxious to hear how your dad did with the wiring, because he heard that your dad tried to fix the

toilet one time and the kitchen sink faucet started running water when anyone flushed the toilet. HO! HO!"

I guess it might be good to let you know at this point that Mrs. Santa loved to tease her little brother, Rine, when they were younger, and she continues to do it today. So part of our fun in writing to Andrew is to keep up that tradition of using humor when it comes to Mrs. Santa's real brother, Rine. Of course, anytime I refer to "your dad" in this letter, you know it is to get the attention of Mrs. Santa's brother, Rine.

"Now, about those spies you think I might have up here at the North Pole....let me tell you that I do not have spies, but I have a lot of Brownie Buzz going on. It seems they just know a lot of things that are going on everywhere. I don't know what I'd do without them.

Andrew, one of my Brownies told me about your saying 'Live in the sunshine.' That is such a good saying and I agree with it. If we focus on the good things in life and keep ourselves in the sunshine, our days will be warm and sunny. You have got the right idea there, that's for sure.

Mrs. Santa laughed when she heard about the guy you thought looked like me that was in the painting video. A lot of people tell me I look like Colonel Sanders, but Mrs. Santa thinks I am much better looking than him. She thinks I'm pretty smart, too, because after all, I did marry her! That was a bright idea, too, wasn't it?

One thing you might want to know, Andrew, is that some of the Brownies also heard that your mom and dad like to do that swing dancing when you turn on your music. I hope they don't get too carried away and throw their backs out. I know that would happen to me if I tried that. Of course, I am a little bit older than them. I think you had better keep your eye on them, though. They aren't as young as they used to be.

Well, I guess I had better go now because Mrs. Santa called me into the kitchen. It seems she has a snack ready for me. I wonder what it will be tonight. Maybe it will be a

snowflake sundae with those great icicle sticks on top. She'll probably have some snowball juice to go with it. Thank you for writing to me. I enjoyed your letter very much. I hope to hear from you again.
Love, Santa."

Two more good friends of mine are Dave and Carol Wenger from York, Pennsylvania. This is a letter I wrote to their daughter.

"Hi Jennifer,
Mrs. Santa just walked through the cabin singing, 'It's Beginning to Look a Lot Like Christmas,' and it really is up here. We have more snow than we know what to do with. Actually, Rudolph and his whole team were out yesterday with their snowblowers just clearing off the sidewalks because Mrs. Santa doesn't like to wear those clumsy snowshoes.

It certainly was nice of you to think of all of the other boys and girls because as you say, you think all children have been wonderful.

I don't know why your brothers and sisters wouldn't believe you when you said you had a mouse because I know you have a Christmas book with a mouse in it. I know that Mrs. Santa has a mouse with her computer. I'll bet your dad has one, too. So you see, there are mice all over the place.

Let me tell you what happened yesterday. I gave the Brownies a little break because they work so hard. The next thing I knew they were out in the front yard riding the reindeer and having a snowball battle. I think Rudolph was having the most fun. He wanted me to let you know that he is taking a shortcut to your house in York this year.

He asked me if he could put his noseprint on your letter. That means it's the same thing as signing his name. You would never be able to read his hoof scratching.

I'll bet you like to go over to Grandpa and Grandma Wenger's in Lancaster. I stopped in to see Grandpa one day because I had a crick in my neck. I knew he was a great chiropractor and he would be able to fix me up, and he sure did. Now Mrs. Santa wants to go to see him because she thinks she hurt her hip when she was working out with the cheerleaders. She calls them her Snowbelles. I never thought I would see the day when Mrs. Santa would get so wrapped up in the fitness center. Would you believe me if I told you she is now pumping iron? The next thing I know I'll have to do some of that just to stay up with her.

Well Jennifer, I have to get this letter over to the post office because I told my Brownie postmaster, Stamper, that I wanted this to go out by special mail.

We're anxious to see your house and I sure was thrilled to get your nicely printed letter. It was so good that the Brownies decided they wanted to send you one of their favorite awards. It's our 'Good Job Award.'
Love, Santa."

Longtime friends of mine, Dan and Lee Miller, from Lititz, Pennsylvania, have two grandchildren, Haley and Trey, who write to me every year. It is with a heavy heart that, at this writing, I must say Grandpa Dan is no longer with us, even though he was here on earth at the time I wrote this answer.

"Hi Haley and Trey,
Boy, are we anxious to see the two of you this year. This will be the first time we see your little brother, Haley. I see he was born in August, too. That was a good month for

your parents. I'll bet you enjoy being a big sister, Haley, because you are so kind. And you always have such a smile on your face. I asked Grandma Lee to send me some pictures of you.

I know Trey does not know anything about me yet, Haley, but someday you will be able to tell him everything. By the way, I liked that little shirt with all the hearts on it and the blue jumper. I can see why Trey would laugh at you a lot because you are such a fun girl. Both of you will be easy to please this year. I know you must have fun taking walks with Grandma Lee. I told Rudolph you go to see the horses sometimes. We have a lot more reindeer up here than horses, but we do have some horses. We need reindeer because of all of the snow and because they are faster and because we can get milk from them. I did want to send you a picture of one of Rudolph's friends and her little colt. Her name is Springer.

Going to the zoo must have really been fun. You should have seen some of Rudolph's cousins there. There are a lot of them. I see your favorite animal is the tiger. We don't have any tigers up here, but since you like them so much, I thought I would send you a sticker of one that is in the South Pole Zoo.

Mrs. Santa's favorite color is purple and mine, of course, is red. But purple is my next favorite color. I think red makes a prettier suit than purple, don't you? I do have a pair of purple jeans that I like a lot. They go very well with my snow boots.

I know all about Grandma Lee's famous sand tarts. I sure hope she leaves a cookie snack for me. I hope Grandpa Dan doesn't eat them all before I get there. Her sand tarts remind me so much of Mrs. Santa's flat snowball cookies. Well, I hear Mrs. Santa calling me right now, so I know I must not keep her waiting. I will see you both on

Christmas Eve. We will take a picture of your tree to show
Mrs. Santa when we get back.
Love, Santa."

Gene and Barb Garrod, from York, Pennsylvania, were instrumental in making sure their nephew Trevor got his letter off to Santa so they could laugh along when Trevor received his answer from me. Gene and Barb are some very special friends of mine, too. Notice the hint for Mommy at the end of the letter. Parents must be 'tuned-in' when I make a subtle suggestion.

"Hi Trevor,
You really know how to get my attention when you use a
red envelope and such neat stickers. Two of your stickers
look like Mrs. Santa and me. And you didn't forget
Rudolph, either, did you? Since you remembered Rudolph,
he wants to remember you. That's why he is putting his
noseprint on your letter.

Your mommy is a really neat printer. I don't usually give
awards for mommies for printing, but Mrs. Santa said she
thought she deserved it. Golly, maybe it was daddy who
did the printing. Either way, it deserves an award.

I certainly do know your Uncle Gene and Aunt Barb. They
are such neat people. They have a nice farm. Did you ever
know that I named my Barbie doll after your Aunt Barb?

I guess it isn't too bad if you are a little naughty once in a
while, but you certainly don't want to make a practice of
it. I am taking your promise seriously that you are going to
be good from now on. You ask Miss Betty if she remembers
writing to me. When she was little and asked for a slate
board, I knew she was going to be a teacher.

The Brownies have been so busy this summer. We got two

new Brownie doctors up here, Dr. Salt and Dr. Pepper. We have two of our girl Brownies studying to be nurses. Their names are Pulsar and Nightingale. They all train at St. Nick's Children's Hospital.

I see you asked for a pair of boxing gloves. The Brownies have a boxing team up here and the head trainer is Pugsy. They wear helmets so they don't seriously hurt each other.

Trevor, if you go up to Uncle Gene's and Aunt Barb's, you might be able to ride a horse. Your Uncle Gene doesn't have any reindeer, though. It is even more fun to ride a reindeer.

Well, I'll be around to see you in about 10 more days, so get things ready for me. Bye now.
Love, Santa.

P.S. I thought since you had a P.S., I would, too. So my P.S. says that Copper will get something from me. You will have to wait and see if it is a bone or if I think of something else. I'm not going to leave it under the tree because he might smell it and go after it before morning. I'll give it a good place where he can't get at it, but you will see it. Doesn't that sound like a good idea, Mommy?"

Other good friends of ours, Glen and Ruth Shultz, of Lancaster, Pennyslvania, gave me quite a bit of information about their grandchildren, which allowed Santa to be absolutely brilliant when answering their letters. Grandpa Glen and Grandma Ruth love to laugh, so I knew they would enjoy the line about the wrinkle cream at the end of the letter.

"Hi Jordan and Megan,
Since it is getting so late, I'll bet you thought I forgot you, but that could never happen. Rudolph told me he found a shortcut to your house in Ephrata and we are going to make it one of our early stops. You know what that

means—go to bed early because I don't stop if you are still up. Mommy can stay up if she wants to and then I'll give her a Santa hug just like I give Grandma Shultz when I see her. I am so glad Grandpa Shultz is feeling better these days. Now he won't have any excuse when he hits a golf ball into the woods.

Jordan, I want to be honest with you. I don't bring front teeth because that is something that your own body will take care of. The next teeth you get will last your whole lifetime. I still have every one of mine and look how old I am. Well, I don't even know how old I am because we don't count birthdays up here.

Megan, I want you to be a little more careful so you don't fall and get so many boo-boos. I think it would be nice if I brought you some new puzzles to put together and that way you will be able to sit still and you won't fall so much. I guess you have fun playing with Courtney and Cassandra at your school. I hope you and Jordan are sharing, Megan, because that makes us happy.

Jordan, I think you are pretty good at making things, so how would you like it if I brought you a toolbox? I know you like to play soccer and I am sending you a picture of one of the Brownie soccer balls. They have a great team and they call themselves the Brownie Booters. They have a goalie, Stretch, who never lets the ball get past him.

I hope the two of you are taking good care of Simon. Rudolph told me to ask you if it would be all right if he brought Simon some special Kitten Kurls. Mrs. Santa wanted me to show you a picture of one of her new cats. She calls her Inky. Inky sleeps a lot. Her tail seems to be the blackest part of her. Maybe she got it in a bucket of black paint over at the paint shop.

You tell Daddy we are going to stop by his Beverage Mart to see if he carries any snowball juice. I drink a lot of that up here because it gives me pep. I guess mommy is still working there at Olde Hickory. I know they have a little golf course there.

Well, my little friends, Mrs. Santa just reminded me that I promised to go over to the Surprise Shop and pick something out for each one of you and for Grandpa and Grandma Shultz. Maybe I'll bring them some wrinkle cream.

I'll see you on Christmas Eve. I'll bring my camera so I can show Mrs. Santa a picture of you and your house.
Love, Santa."

Of course, most of the letters that I receive are not from friends and family. I often get letters from schools, hospitals and nursing homes. Following a speaking engagement in western Pennsylvania, I received a letter from the residents at the Good Samaritan Nursing Care Home. Since I answer every letter I receive, I was happy to send this reply to my new friends.

"To all my friends at Good Samaritan,
You don't know how much joy you brought to my heart when your letter arrived. I am glad you were talking about me and then did something about it by writing to me. You know I will have a Merry Christmas because of folks like you, as well as your little friends who come to you with their magic moments."

The reason for mentioning "magic moments" is because there are some children who visit the residents in the nursing home and they are called the "Magic Moments." They have an exchange program, which I think is pretty neat. What a great way to bridge the generation gap. Everyone wins.

"My greatest wish to all of you is that God continues to watch over you and lighten your load. Remember, He never

gives anyone a load too heavy for them to carry. Treating the children well is an easy wish to fulfill. I know Linda will get some candy canes."

Linda is one of the elderly residents who wanted some candy canes.

"I am going to ask my friend, Ann, to see to that."

Ann is an aide who works at the nursing home.

"I want her to have them now so they are fresh, so I'm sending a little cash to make that happen. I'm sure Linda will share her candy canes with you.

I wish I could keep the world in peace as you requested. If everyone had the real spirit of Christmas, this wouldn't be a problem. We must learn to get along with each other. I am sending you one of my Smiley Faces as a reminder of how the corners of our mouths should turn. Remember that 'when you are smiling, the whole world smiles with you.' If I could be there with you we would sing that song together. I'm sure you would know the words. If you didn't know the words, we would hum them. That's what Mrs. Santa does. She hums them when she doesn't know the words. Incidentally, Mrs. Santa has a project up here at the North Pole. She instituted what she calls the 'Humming Choir' for all the Brownies who can't remember the words. They just hum. That way they feel they are a part of things. I wish it were possible for me to be with you, but you know what I'm doing these days. Mrs. Santa and I want you to know that we are with you in spirit. God loves you and so do we.
  Love, Santa."

Sometimes we find that children have a special way of closing the generation gap. So, this next answer was sent to the children who spent time with the Good Samaritan residents.

*"Dear Boys and Girls,
I hope you are not too disappointed, but when I get letters
from school classes, I can only take time to write one long
letter for the teacher to read to the whole class, so I will
ask Miss Jody to read my letter to you. There are just too
many boys and girls in schools to write a letter to each of
them. I am sure you can understand that. I read each one of
your letters, though, and I sure do know the color of your
houses."*

Each child mentioned the color of his or her house. One of them was black and blue.
I don't know that I've ever seen one quite like that. I guess it must have been hit
with some wind, rain, or snow!

*"Rudolph has every one of your houses in his big 'Never
Forget Address Book.' He told me we are going to start
our trip in the Johnstown area this year and that means
you should go to bed a little earlier. Mrs. Santa asked me
to bring my camera along so I could take pictures of you
while you are sleeping. She never gets a chance to see any
of my little friends, but she will this year. The Brownies
made me one of their famous Brownie cameras. I know
you all will have smiles on your faces, because you will be
thinking of me and what will be under the tree when you
get up.*

*Oh, Mrs. Santa just called to tell me she wanted you to
have one of her special awards because of the good things
you do with the older residents at the Good Samaritan. We
don't miss much up here. We love your 'Magic Moments'
program. She will put the 'Bright Idea Award' at the
bottom of the page.*

We start a lot of things up here at the North Pole and

eventually they get down there. Sure—you know your 'Meals on Wheels' program? Rudolph started that up at the North Pole. He called it 'Fed from a Sled.' We specialize in bright ideas up here. Each January, we have an Idea Fair to see which Brownie has the best idea for the Christmas season. We got some humdingers this year. We even got one that was a lollapalooza. They are pretty scarce. I got Mrs. Santa a thinking cap three years ago and she gets some of the brightest ideas now. I should have gotten her that a long time ago. HO! HO! If she hears me say that, she will pull my whiskers! Well, she must have had her thinking cap on when she married me, don't you think? HO! HO! That was one of the brightest ideas she ever had.

Rudolph is adding two more reindeer to the team this year. You are getting in on some big ground floor news here. Their names are Sunny and Beamer. He tells me his load is getting too heavy. I hope he didn't mean me! Well, I'm running out of paper. Remember to say your prayers. Bye now. Love, Santa."

The Brownies serve as role models for the children. They eat their fruits and vegetables and they all have chores to do. If a child's mother writes and tells me that little Pammy is having trouble eating the vegetables on her plate, I'll write, "Pammy, if you want to become a member of the 'Eat 'em Clean Club' that the Brownies have up here, then you had better eat all those vegetables on your plate." And then I will get a letter back from the mother saying, "You wouldn't believe it. She is eating everything on her plate, including her vegetables!"

That gives you a "flavor" of the kinds of answers I write, doesn't it?

We all have gifts to give others, and they don't necessarily come wrapped in paper. What all of us truly need is to be wrapped in love, kindness, and compassion. Someone you know needs some encouragement, and someone to lend an ear. And in some cases, they need you to offer them hope and help them with their dreams.

Many years ago, Edward Everett Hale, a chaplain in the United States Senate said this:

"I am but one, but I am one. I cannot do everything, but I can do something. What I can do, I ought to do, and what I ought to do, by the grace of God, I will do."

We all have that same choice. Obviously, I don't know all of the more than 100,000 children to whom I have written, and I will never see them all. However, my heart tells me that I might have put smiles on their faces.

It is never too soon to do a kindness. Look around you. A little thing could make a big difference in someone's life. Believe me, you have that power.

Chapter Seven
Tender, Touching and Tearful

Over many years of corresponding with my little friends, there have been some very tender and touching letters—letters that demonstrate hope, kindness, joy, curiosity, love, courage, compassion and, yes, heartbreak. These letters are a reminder that life is not always full of joy and peace, nor is it free of tragedy. They also are a reminder that we should learn to embrace the good and let go of the bad and remember to never give up hope.

There is much to learn when bad things happen to good people. So often, we are inspired to open our hearts and provide help to others when tragedy strikes. The Good Samaritan spirit is a reminder for all of us to reach out to those who are suffering in one way or another.

I reach out with words of comfort and hope when I receive letters that touch my heart, or worse, leave me heartbroken. I get a great deal of joy and consolation when parents tell me, on occasion, just how much my small labor of love has done for their child as well as them when they needed it most.

Following are some examples of letters that have touched me deeply. The first one is an example of heartbreak followed by joy.

After I gave a talk to a group of nurses in York, Pennsylvania, a woman came forward and asked me if I would write a letter to her nephew. She said there were some special circumstances surrounding the situation, and I said that would be fine because challenges were not new to me.

She told me her nephew was going to be entering the Hershey Medical Center in Hershey, Pennsylvania, for a heart operation. He had a hole in his heart and needed surgery within two days. She thought it would be so uplifting to him if he could receive a letter from Santa Claus before his surgery.

I knew there wasn't enough time to send the letter in the mail, so I called my friend, Karen, who was the Admissions Director at the hospital. I explained the situation and asked if she would hand carry the letter to the little boy that day, if I brought it to the hospital. She graciously agreed and little Titus from Tower City, Pennsylvania, a small mountainous town north of Harrisburg, received the following letter.

"Dear Titus,

I know you might be a little bit concerned about your operation, but I want you to know that I think everything will be fine. Let me tell you why I say that. Up here at the North Pole, we have a prayer circle and it is called the Brownie Prayer Circle. When Mrs. Santa and I and all of the Brownies know that someone has a problem, we all get together and hold hands in our prayer circle, praying to God that things will turn out okay. I can tell you that is a lot of 'prayer power' when we all get together and pray for the same thing. I am sure things will be fine, Titus.
Love, Santa."

Now, if you have never believed in miracles before, just read the following letter to learn what happened the day of the operation. It is obvious Titus's mother was writing this letter for her son; however, I do believe the warmth and gratitude come from both of them.

"Dear Santa,

My name is Titus. I'm 3 years old now. You probably remember me because Mrs. Santa, the brownie troop and you were praying about my heart. Well, Santa, God heard our prayers. The hole in my heart closed by God's hand. A miracle happened to me. The doctors at Hershey Medical Center did not have to operate on my heart. I got this good news in March of 1995. I was completely discharged from the hospital as well on that same day in March.

I'm still sleeping with Baby Big Bird that you brought to me on December 25. He is getting old, but Mommy keeps him looking clean and like brand new. She puts him in a pillowcase and washes and drys him for me. She uses the washer and dryer. Big Bird gets a bath about once a month. Daddy fixes his eyes with a magic marker, black.

Well, Santa, here is my list for you and your elves. Red wagon, tool box and tools, grill, Fisher-Price cars and trucks. Thank you, Santa. Remember, Santa, that there will be carrots for the reindeer and cookies for you on the kitchen table.
Love, Titus.
P.S. Santa, you are great because God is your copilot."

True happiness has continued for Titus. After a few years, I heard from his mother again and he was doing fine. In fact, his family was going on a vacation to Disney World, since this was something he had wished for.

However, that is not the end of the story. There is a benefit I really did not anticipate. Titus now tells everyone he knows who has to go to the hospital for an operation, "You should not worry because I am going to tell Santa Claus and his Brownies to put you in their prayer circle and things will turn out fine."

When I heard that, I just had to believe Titus was perpetuating the powerful benefits of prayer and helping to put other people at ease. I wonder if Titus realizes he has become a "missionary of hope" for many others. What a nice title for "Little Titus."

On occasion, a letter will give me a sense of uneasiness. Such is the case with this next one.

"Dear Santa,
This is Xavier. Hey, my phone number is...My mother is gone and my grandmother is taking care of me and my sister. I live in Palmdale, California."

He went on to write his wish list; however, it was the first part of his letter that concerned me, so I decided to try to find out if I could lift him up with my response.

"Hi Xavier,
I think it was a nice surprise that you wrote to me this year. I think this is the first time I heard from you. Or

maybe you wrote to one of my helpers and didn't write directly to me.

I just looked out the window, and it is snowing up here again. I know this would be something new in Palmdale, but it happens up here all the time. Actually, we like snow a lot. Rudolph just loves to run around and then look at his tracks to see where he has been.

I see you are into basketball and so are we up here. My Brownies had a game last night. We do have to give them some time to play since they work so hard all of the time. Their team is called the Happy Hoopsters and they are terrific! You know my Brownies aren't very tall, so they make up for this by doing trick shots. They jump on each other's shoulders and do slam dunks. Sometimes they just run between the legs of their opponents to confuse them. We have one Brownie basketball player who took lessons from Michael Jordan, because he wanted to be like Mike. His name is Swish. When he shoots, all you hear is the swish when the ball goes through the net.

I see you wear a size 10 shoe. I think Mrs. Santa wears a size 6 1/2, but I know hers is not a kid size.

It was pretty nice of your grandmother to take care of you since your mother was gone. I'll bet your grandmother does a lot of nice things for you. I hope you remember to give her a hug. I remember when your grandmother used to write to me. I think she sent me her picture one time. That might be a good idea for you to do if you write to me next year. See you Christmas Eve.
Love, Santa."

My thought was that if Xavier could focus on the good in his life, then perhaps it would make things just a little easier for him. I also wanted to fill my letter to him with lots of fun so he could remember to smile.

The same holds true when I receive letters, such as those on the next page, from children with other problems or hardships. One is from a child who is concerned about her parents fighting. Another is from a child who believes Christmas won't be the same because his parents are in debt. The third is from a child who wants peace between mom and dad.

Doesn't this just tug at your heart? It is so sad that little children have such burdens in their early years. I can let the child know that I am thankful they were able to tell me of the hurt they were feeling. This may be the only outlet they have and they feel safe discussing it with Santa Claus.

11\27\02

Dear Santa
I wish that you could make my parents not get in too many fights any more. Last year I got that Scoot scooter that you gave me. Santa, please get my letter because I really want my parents to stop fightsing for doust a little o bit. And please get someone to fix ragged Ann.
Love Your frena

Dear Santa,
I hope you don't get sick again for Cristmas I hope I get Gooze or something squooshy! Maybe a Marvin Redpost book. I like Marvin. I'm reading one. My mom and dad are in debt so Cristmas will not be the same.

One thing I want is some
peace between Mom and Dad.
I also want a camera that you don't
throw away after you use it one time.
I hope you have a good christmas.
Love from your friend,

As for the child who believes Christmas won't be the same because his parents are in debt, I can only remind him that money does not always make the best Christmas. I can encourage him to do nice things for others and that will make him feel a whole lot better because that is truly the Spirit of Christmas. Of course, tactfully, I will suggest to the parents that they be more aware of the example they are setting for their children.

Here is a tender letter from Christina, who has quite a bit on her plate. Although she seems to be a troubled child, you will hear the goodness within her because it is apparent in her letter to Santa. As Santa and as a parent, I try to understand, encourage and share some wisdom.

> *"Dear Santa,*
> *I've never really believed in you when I was a little kid.*
> *There's only one way to know if you're real. This is what*
> *I want for Christmas. A violin and contacts for my eyes*
> *instead of glasses. I've been a little out of hand this year*
> *and that's why I'm in a Youth Development Center. In*
> *January I'm going somewhere so I can get help with my*
> *problems. I'm going to change into a better person and I've*
> *already started working on it. It's coming along good so*
> *far. I hold the Spirit of Christmas within my heart, but all*
> *I know is there was a Santa a long time ago known as Kris*
> *Kringle and he died. If you're real, fill me in on some info*
> *and send my presents since I've been trying so hard to be*
> *good. Can you make sure all the needy people get a little*
> *something too? Thanks. Merry Christmas.*
> *Your friend, Christina."*

Sometimes Mrs. Santa receives a tender letter addressed to her. Carly wrote,

"Dear Mrs. Santa,
You probably don't know who I am, but my name is Carly.
I've never written to you before, but I'd like to get to know
you. I have hazel eyes, shoulder length hair, brown hair
by the way, and small freckles. I think Santa Claus gets a
lot of letters and you deserve at least one letter. I would
enjoy it if you would be my pen pal. You don't have to if
you don't want to, but I decided to ask you because Santa
Claus is always so busy. Have a Merry Christmas and a
Happy New Year.
Love, Carly."

Now I know Mrs. Santa Claus was touched by this letter and sat down and wrote to Carly. She said, "I would love to be your pen pal." Unfortunately, that's the last time we heard from Carly. I do think Carly had good intentions at the time.

This next little guy, Scott, was 12 years old on December 13, 2006, when he underwent a very serious heart operation at The Children's Hospital of Philadelphia. We were all very concerned about him having this serious operation, but of course, it was necessary. The surgeons actually took Scott's heart out, carved it down to size, and put it back in. Within three days, Scott was able to walk around, which in Santa's eyes, is a miracle.

Scott is known for giving hugs and big smiles to everyone. His attitude is one that we should all have. The operation was a success and since it was around Christmastime, Santa was compelled to write him this letter.

"Hi Scott,
Well, you have been through a whirlwind this Christmas,
haven't you? I want you to know that our big Brownie
prayer circle has had you on their list for some time now.
They knew you were going to have this big heart operation
and they wanted everything to turn out well for you. We
have a lot of Brownie power up here and when they heard
how well you did, they actually cried. I must say that Mrs.
Santa and I had tears of joy, too. When Happy, one of the

Brownies up here, ran over to the Reindeer Ranch to tell Rudolph, Happy told me later that Rudolph and the other reindeer began clacking their hoofs and cheering so loud. Now I know what all that racket was that I heard when I was sitting in my cabin. Happy even saw Rudolph wipe a tear away from his eye. And you can imagine how big a reindeer's tear is!

We all sat around the campfire last night and talked all about you. We heard some stories about how smart you are about your heart. The Brownies are just sure you will be carrying a stethoscope around your neck when you grow up. We all knew about your warm heart, Scott, but now we understand you have some warm fingers and toes, thanks to your doctors. I'll bet that feels good since you haven't had that for a long time. I know it does for me up here where it is so cold. Mrs. Santa surprised me last year with a pair of those fuzzy wool socks. Boy, are they great. And, of course, you know they are red because that is my favorite color.

We are going to bring something very special for all the doctors and nurses down there at that Children's Hospital of Philadelphia where you had your operation. They help make miracles happen, don't they? And you are one of them. Of course, we were also praying for your mom, Linda, and your dad, Mark, and all the rest of your family and those who love you, too, because we know how much they love you and how concerned all of them were. You are such a bright spot for so many people, Scott. You just keep being yourself.

Mrs. Santa is over at the Surprise Shop working on a surprise for you right now as I am writing this letter. I think she wants to wrap it in all red paper. You will have to look for it Christmas morning. Doesn't that sound like a good idea, Mother?

Scott, it will be no time before you can give those great bear hugs again. I know you have to give little tender hugs right now, but that will change before you know it. I want you to know that all of us up here are sending our hugs your way. If you ever feel a warm blast, that will be it. That's how Mrs. Santa and I keep warm—we give lots of hugs. She says my hugs are the best hugs. But, then, she never had one of yours, so yours might be as good as mine.

Well, Scott, I guess I had better get this letter in the mail to you since it is so close to the big day. We'll be traveling on the Milky Way for a while, but we will spend a lot of time on Cloud Nine. We like it there. This year we are going to use the North Star to guide us most of the way. With the different time zones, I don't think we'll have any trouble making it to all the stops.

If you are thinking of leaving me a snack, I would really appreciate one of those energy drinks or an energy bar. I'll need some energy by the time I get to your house.

Keep smiling, keep giving hugs, and keep getting better and better and better and better and better and better and better and better and better and better until you are feeling your... BEST!!! I'll be seeing you Christmas Eve. Bye now. Love, Santa."

A girl named Heather began her letter by listing all the material things she wanted for Christmas, but then she wrote a sentence that created a lump in my throat. You will know exactly what I mean when you read it.

"Dear Santa,
I would like a car, truck, for Christmas. I would like potato chips and gummy worms. I would like to have my cancer fixed. Please bring my dad a horse for his window. It has to be green. And he likes tool stuff.
Thanks, Heather."

In my answer, I tried to assure Heather that everything would turn out okay. I replied,

"Dear Heather,
I am so glad you wrote to me early this year. That really
helps me a lot because then I can send you an early answer.

Since you live in Hanover, you must know that you have
the best potato chips in the country. I always bring some
back for Mrs. Santa. She likes the Utz's regular light chips.
I guess she thinks she will be lighter if she eats lighter
potato chips. I know Snyder's in Hanover has good potato
chips, too. And I like their pretzels. I wonder if you know
that the man who started Utz's Potato Chips started his
factory on McAllister Street, not far from where you live.
He was a nice man named Bill Utz.

It sounds like your dad likes to fix things, so I guess he
could use a few new tools. I'll have to talk to him about
that horse for his window. I know it has to be green, but I
don't know much else about it.

Heather, I know you said you would like to have your
cancer fixed. This is what I am going to do. I have a very
good friend whose name is God. And I talk to Him every
day. He would be the best person I know to help you with
this problem. He oftentimes works with doctors to help
them with these problems.

I see you don't have a very long list this year, and that is
thoughtful of you. I try to have enough presents for all the
little boys and girls, so I must make sure there is something
for everyone.

I just looked out my window and it is snowing again
up here. I know you haven't had any snow in Hanover

yet, but I think you will before I come around on my big trip. I know Rudolph will want to stop at the Hanover Horse Farm again this year and visit some of his 'horsey' friends. We will all be praying for you, Heather. I'll see you Christmas Eve.
Love, Santa."

The following letter from Greg was a ray of sunshine. I received his letter after presenting my "Letters to Santa" talk to an Intermediate School. I had a warm feeling when I read this nice letter from Greg, who was part of this group. I hope Greg carries this change of thinking throughout his life. It does sound like he has been hit with some arrows of disappointment in his life.

"Dear Santa,
I am 12 years old. I've never written to Santa before. Just recently you came in to my school to talk about your winter profession. I think it's wonderful what you do. It sounds like a lot of fun (which I'm sure it is), but I'm positive it's a lot of work.

Before you came in to my school, I didn't really think there were any good-natured people in the world. By that, I mean when people do something for others they always expect something in return. When you came you changed my way of thinking. I'm glad!"

I'm glad, too, because it sounds like Greg was happy to find out not everyone is looking for something in return.

"I just want to thank you for sharing your time and experiences and I wish you many more years of writing.
MERRY CHRISTMAS!
Your friend, Greg."

It is obvious by this letter that Greg wants more out of life and may just need some encouragement from others.

What Debra is looking for is also obvious, even if the reason is not quite so transparent. She wrote:

"Dear Santa,
For Christmas I would like A Easy Bake Oven, Ken doll
and accessories, one horse book, 6 pair knee stockings, 4
pair ankle stockings, and Love."

It just seemed clear to me that Debra was searching for love since it was the only thing that was underscored in red. Since I am so close to these children, I guess a couple of thoughts ran through my mind. One, why did the child write the need for love and underscore it? Could it be the child was not receiving love and was starved for affection? Or possibly, did she just feel that Santa had a special brand of love? I don't really know the answer. I do know this, however. I hope it was the latter. You can be sure I put as much love as possible in that answer when I responded to her letter.

Another heartbreaking letter was actually a memorial card with the photo of one of my "little ones" who was taken to her Heavenly home early in her life. In 1978, I received an announcement of a Mass being held for a little girl by the name of Lynn. Inside that announcement was a note from Lynn's mother, which said,

"Dear Santa,
Lynn was starting to make her list for you when she was
killed by a car—right in front of our home. I thought you
might like to see what she looked like after so many years
of giving her joy. She so looked forward to your letter at
Christmas and birthday time. Thank you for making her
short life a little happier.
With love, Jane, Lynn's mother."

Unfortunately, there was no return address on the letter. The only bit of help for me was the postmark, which was Southeastern Pennsylvania. At that time, the postmark didn't really tell me the town it was coming from. This was just a post office somewhere in that area.

I was giving a talk one night to a small chapter of the Lion's Club in Smoketown, Pennsylvania. It so happened that a friend of mine, Faith, was the postmaster in this small town. I told the audience how much it would mean to me if I could somehow or another track down Jane and get in touch with her.

Faith came up to me after my talk and said she wanted to help. She said she was going to go back to the post office to see how many post offices operated under the Southeastern postmark. She did that and found out there were 72 post offices at that time. She took it upon herself to send a letter to each of the postmasters in each of those 72 post offices simply asking the question, "Do you have Lynn's parents on your route?"

t was just a matter of days when she received a response from the postmaster of King of Prussia, Pennsylvania, saying that he knew the family. He had known of the tragedy that took Lynn's life. I certainly was grateful to Faith for taking on this act of kindness. Now I could respond to the mother because I had her full address.

I felt that any mother who would take the time to write to Santa Claus about her believing daughter deserved a response from me. I asked how she knew about me as Santa Claus. She said she had attended a conference in Philadelphia, Pennsylvania, for mothers of adopted children and I was the speaker. She said she was so taken by my endeavors writing to children that she and Lynn started to write letters to me. So, obviously, Lynn was an adopted child and certainly one whose mother loved her dearly.

This letter from Laura is another one that will break your heart. She wrote,

> *"Santa Clauz,*
> *All I want for Crismas iz another Daddy because my*
> *Daddy is ded. Last year my mommy cried because she*
> *could not put up the Christmas tree alone. And the tree*
> *fell down because it was not up right. And I also miss my*
> *Daddy. I am almost seven years old. My brother is helping*
> *me. So please send me a Daddy and remembre me at X-mas.*
> *Thank you, Laura.*
> *P.S. I have been good all year."*

Keep in mind that I get very close to these kids. I have been with them through the Korean War, Vietnam War, Desert Storm and now Iraq. On one occasion I received a letter from a child saying,

> *"All I want for Christmas is for my daddy to come home."*

And then the mother sent a little note with a P.S. that said, "Daddy is never coming home because he was killed in action." At times like this, Santa realizes his inability to always say the proper things without asking for the right words from his Heavenly Father. Then the words seem to flow like a gift from Heaven.

Believe me, I am often inspired by the devotion of the parents to their children. Randy, father of three, in York, Pennsylvania, is such a person. This year Randy's daughter, Jackie, wrote her own letter and it was such a thoughtful one. Jackie is a very bright and caring young lady, as you will note from a few questions in her letter to Santa.

She wanted to know why homeless people don't get presents from Santa Claus. When I responded to her, I did make it clear that we give them every opportunity to have a roof over their heads, warm meals, and a bed in which to sleep. Another of Jackie's questions was, "Why do rich children get more presents than poor children?" I told her I do not think of children as being rich or poor. They are all God's children and mine, too. I further explained that sometimes, rich children get presents from other people who feel the need to please them. We should be more concerned about what we need and not quite as concerned with what we want.

In her letter Jackie described herself as a "fashion queen." From her requests, I could figure that out for myself. When she sent her picture to me, it was evident that she fit the part. She made sure I had her cell phone number and requested that I call her to prove that I was real. I know Jackie had reached the age of being "on the fence." I made that phone call from Santa Claus and we had a great conversation. What a nice young lady, and what a caring father she has in Randy. Oh, yes, I also wrote to her older brothers for a number of years.

All beautiful journeys have special memorable events. And Sally's letter is a very special one. I suppose it is my favorite letter and I'm not sure why. After you read it you might have your own answer. It certainly was different.

> *"Dear Santa Claus,*
> *All I want from you this year is a walking doll. The reason*
> *I want a walking doll is because I got polio in August and*
> *I will never be able to walk again. Do you think you could*
> *bring me a doll that walks? I've really tried to be good.*
> *Sally, age 7."*

No last name—no return address—dropped in the mailbox of the log cabin on Center Square in Hanover. I wanted to write an optimistic letter to Sally and I went through all kinds of torment wondering how I could get an answer to this child. I had about three sleepless nights, believe me. Finally I thought, "There has to be a way."

When I need help, I know where to look. So I asked, "What is the right thing to do here?" And then it clicked. My neighbor was the editor of the Hanover Evening Sun newspaper. I took Sally's letter to him and said, "Ed, I've got to answer this. Would you print this letter on your front page? I will give you an answer to her letter."

He printed that letter on the front page with my answer, which said,

> *"Sally,*
> *I got your letter but I must tell you something I have never*
> *told anyone before. I think I forgot your last name and*
> *I can't remember your address. Yes, I am getting a little*

older. I usually depend on Rudolph because he has all this information in his big address book but he is not here right now. He is down at the South Pole training a couple of Greenies to become Brownies and he won't be back for a little bit. Then when he comes back, he will need to go to the North Woods for some fireplace wood because it is so cold up here and my supply is getting low. I really don't want to wait until he comes back to answer your letter, so Sally, will you please send me another letter and include your last name and your address?"

Since I am writing directly to Sally, I am hoping someone who knows Sally will read the letter on the front page of the newspaper and pick up on this. I went on to comfort Sally by saying,

"I know how you feel, Sally. One of my Brownies got polio in August and I know how he felt. He was down in the dumps and he didn't think this was fair. He was trying to do good things for people and he wondered why this had to happen. I had to talk with him and tell him that you didn't have to walk to help other people. So he asked one of his Brownie buddies over in the workshop if he would make him a pair of crutches. Of course his Brownie friend was happy to do it. Now he is walking today and we nicknamed him Sunshine because he is always singing and whistling. Maybe the same thing can happen to you. I'm going to bring you that walking doll so that perhaps someday, somewhere, you and your walking doll will walk together."

Keep in mind, this is the first time I ever promised a child anything. Somehow it just felt right. A week went by and I didn't hear from Sally or her parents. I used a follow-up letter in the newspaper with this heading, "Sally Remains on Santa's Unknown List." Still, there was no answer from Sally. Surely I thought someone, perhaps a relative or a neighbor, would read the letter and recognize Sally. I must

say this was not the happiest Christmas Santa Claus ever had. The lights were taken down, the decorations put away, and the spirit of Christmas was fading.
Then on January 6, another letter came in. It read,

"Dear Santa Claus,
We want to thank you for the kindness offered at the time
we needed it most. The reason you never heard from Sally
again is because she died December 22. But Santa Claus,
we want you to know that we got her a walking doll
on December 21. We knew her time was coming and we
wanted her to have her walking doll. Sally died with a
smile on her face because Santa brought her a walking doll
and she knew that sometime, someplace, somehow she and
her walking doll would walk together. We don't know who
you are, Santa Claus, but thank you. Whoever you are,
don't ever stop writing letters to children.
Sally's mother."

So the original letter, which was dropped in Santa's box on Center Square in Hanover, was from Manchester, Maryland—from a mother and daughter who believed in Santa Claus. Oh, the tender experiences I've had. To this day, they still bring a tear to my eye.

Chapter Eight
Santa's Final Word

We believe Christmas is the most beautiful time of the year—not just up here at the North Pole but the world over. We realize all too well the true meaning of Christmas is the birth of Jesus, not Santa in a red suit bringing presents to children around the globe. However, that doesn't mean children can't believe in more than one person they cannot see.

Perhaps a young girl named Chloe said it best. She is a child who dearly loves Jesus but still believes in Santa Claus, too. With her parents laying the proper foundation, it is clear that Chloe has no trouble distinguishing between Jesus and Santa Claus.

She did not ask for anything at all for herself. It was just important to her to get this message to Jesus.

> *"Dear Santa, Please give this to God. God, please give this to Jesus on December 25th. Happy Birthday. Love, Chloe."*

Then at the bottom she drew in outlined letters,

> *"Jesus! 2004. Jesus. Happy Birthday."*

Santa and Mrs. Santa—along with the entire North Pole family—wish all of you a Happy Life and a Merry Christmas every day of the year!

Epilogue
Attitude and Gratitude

When I taught classes to Amish families in Lancaster County some years ago, I included a session that emphasized an "attitude of gratitude." I asked the parents and all of their children to sit in a circle and write a list of everything for which they were thankful. I asked them to post the lists at home as a daily reminder and to add to those lists each day as they thought of other things for which they were thankful.

Not only did they learn from me, I learned firsthand from one of the families I had in class when the Nickel Mine tragedy happened in Lancaster Country. This family, who lost a daughter and had another who was severely wounded, taught me about grace and forgiveness. I would say they had an "attitudinal" state of mind to be able to forgive.

As adults, all of us should keep an "Attitude of Gratitude" list on our refrigerators. It might help us be more like a gentleman I knew late in the 1950s. Larry Sherwood was one of the greatest examples of a man who was grateful for his blessings, despite his blindness.

I met him when I was in New York City to deliver a talk in one of the leading hotels. I was in the lobby when I accidentally bumped into him. When I turned around, I noticed he was carrying a white cane. I immediately said, "I'm sorry. I wasn't looking where I was going." He replied, "That's okay. Neither was I."

There was something about the grin on his face and the way he said those words that led me to believe this was someone I would like to know better, so I introduced myself. Then he said to me, "Well, my name is Larry Sherwood from Rotterdam Junction in New York."

Larry and I struck up a conversation, and we found that we were both there to speak to different audiences. I expressed my interest in hearing him deliver his talk and he said he thought he could arrange that.

Well, I went to hear his talk and I will never forget it. The title was "Intrinsic Values of Life." He spoke about how blessed he thought he was. I made up my mind at that point that I wanted to bring Larry Sherwood to Pennsylvania, to speak to the Pennsylvania Jaycees, of which I was president at the time.

When I called him about coming to Lancaster, I introduced myself and said, "Larry, I'd like you to come to Pennsylvania, to speak to a group of young men, ages 21 to 26. Do you think that is possible?" In his clever and humorous way, he said, "Well, Grover, it would help if you told me the date you would like me to speak."

After I provided Larry with the date and he checked his calendar, he said, "Grover, you are really fortunate. I can make it on that date." I gratefully said, "That's terrific, Larry. I'm so glad you are free." With a slight pause, Larry said to me, "Free? I don't think I said anything about being free. I think I am reasonable and I am available."

Of course, I laughed and we both knew that Larry was going to be coming to Pennsylvania.

He said he would come by train, and I said, "Fine. Larry, if you will give me the schedule, I'll come to the depot to meet you when you get off the train." He said, "That's a good idea, Grover. That's probably where the train will come in." We both had a nice laugh again.

On the designated date, I went down to the depot and, sure enough, that is where the train came in. I wanted to be right where Larry would get off the train because I knew he did not use a guide dog and I wanted to be there to help him. Unfortunately, Larry got off the train about two cars away from where I was standing.

Immediately I just threw up my arm and said rather loudly, "Hi Larry. Grover Gouker here." Larry said, "Well anyone can see that, Grover. Why are you yelling? It's my eyes that don't work. My hearing is terrific!" He immediately started walking toward me and I began walking toward him.

As we met, I asked, "Larry, how was the trip?"

"Oh," he said, "Grover, this is not easy for me to say. I come from upstate New York, but as I was coming down into Pennsylvania, I saw the most beautiful sights. I saw round rolling hills and green grass. And some of the people still have some of the old customs here." I am sure he was talking about the Amish farmers.

He continued by saying, "It was just gorgeous." And then he asked me, "Have you ever seen it, Grover?" I answered him with an honest reply. "Larry, I probably haven't seen it the way you have." Larry told me, "You ought to take the time to appreciate what Mother Nature has done out there. It is beautiful work."

Then Larry told me he was hungry. He said, "It must be about 2 o'clock." I looked at my watch and, sure enough, it was about two minutes after 2 p.m. Larry went on to ask, "Do you have hamburgers in Pennsylvania?" I said, "We do on special occasions." Of course, Larry wanted to know if this was a special occasion and I assured him it was, indeed, a very special occasion. And so we got our hamburgers.

As we were sitting together eating our late lunch, Larry asked, "Grover, will you tell me about the audience tonight?" I replied, "I sure will. The event is one of our quarterly board meetings and there will be about three or four hundred young fellows between the ages of 21 and 36." And then Larry asked, "What time does this begin?" I told him the dinner would be at 7 p.m.

He asked me, "How do you want to work out the time?" I replied, "Well, why don't I just come up to your room about 10 minutes before seven and I'll just knock on the door." With that familiar grin Larry said, "Yes, do that. Then if you have any trouble getting down to the ballroom where I am scheduled to speak, I'll be able to help you." Once again I smiled.

Later, when I knocked on his door he said, "Just give me a second or two, Grover, and I'll get my key." Within a minute, he came out of the room and took me over to the elevator. Without hesitation, he pressed the button for the ballroom. I have had occasion to work with blind people and I have spoken at their conventions. I have found they happen to be ingenious in so many ways.

When we arrived at the ballroom, I told Larry I would be sitting beside him at the head table and that I'd be introducing him to the audience. He said, "That's fine. But, Grover, they didn't come here to hear you speak, so make it short!"

He had such a great sense of humor and I enjoyed his company so much. When it was time for him to speak after the dinner, I followed Larry's advice. I stood up and simply announced, "Ladies and gentlemen—Larry Sherwood." Larry looked in my direction and gave me "two thumbs up." I guess he was satisfied with my introduction.

Larry went on tell the audience about some of the things he had dealt with in his life. He said, "Many people tend to pity me. I certainly don't need pity. Someone recently asked me, 'Larry, why do you go to Yankee Stadium to watch the ball game when you know you can't see it?'

So I answered him by telling him that nobody has to tell me when the hot dog man is coming around with the mustard. I am going to be the first one to know. And nobody has to tell me if the ball is going to clear the fence when the ball hits Mickey Mantle's bat. I will be the first one to know that answer. I will be able to tell at the crack of the bat. I almost feel sorry for you people who have to wait to see if it clears the fence." And then he went on and gave example after example of how fortunate he thought he was.

The last time I talked with Larry he told me he was downtown standing on a street corner. He said to me, "Someone came up to me, tapped me on the shoulder and offered to help me cross the street. So I went to the other side of the street. When I got there, I waited a minute and then turned around and faced the other side of the street.

I knew it would not be long before someone else would ask me if they could help me across the street. Since I didn't want to go across the street in the first place, now I would be back where I wanted to be. But you know," he said, "it was okay because it made two people happy who thought they helped me." What a guy! What an attitude!

Someone asked Larry one time, "Larry, have you been blind all your life?" And Larry's reply was, "Not yet." He was blind all of his life, but don't you see what he meant by, "Not yet?"

I thought it was amusing when Larry told me about a friend with whom he exchanged Christmas presents every year. His friend was deaf and Larry told me he gave him a cassette player one year and, of course, his friend couldn't hear it. Larry's friend then gave him a flashlight, for which he obviously had no need. How wonderful it was for them to share this terrific sense of humor.

There are so many lessons to be learned from people like Larry Sherwood and I was privileged to know him. Larry always found a reason to be grateful for something. Imagine if all of us lived our lives with Larry's attitude.

More recently I met a young man, Dave Musser, who also displays a tremendous positive attitude. He owns a sports card business, and as I mentioned previously, I sometimes send sports cards to children if they show an interest in a particular athlete or team.

After I received a letter from a little boy who was a big fan of Ben Roethlisburger, the Pittsburgh Steelers quarterback, I visited Dave's shop to pick up one of his cards. I told Dave about my "children's ministry" and he immediately offered to supply me with any cards I might need to carry on this tradition.

I found Dave to be a very interesting person. He told me he started saving sports cards as a very young lad and by the time he was eight years old, he was making money selling baseball cards to other children on the school bus. He credits his grandmother for encouraging him in his start of collecting baseball cards as well as teaching him good work ethics. He continued this practice and today he has a thriving business.

Along the way, Dave had an unfortunate accident that put him in a wheelchair. That never deterred him from starting his business, which has been in existence 21 years.

Dave is just another reminder of the power of a positive attitude and the ways in which all of us can reach out and touch someone else.

So is my memory of a child I met nearly six decades ago. I will always recall my meeting with this young boy as one of the nicest Christmas experiences I ever had in my life.

The year was 1950 and I was president of the Jaycees in my hometown of Hanover, Pennsylvania. One of our annual projects was to bus children, ages six to nine, in from the two orphanages in neighboring towns and treat them to what we called an orphan's shopping tour.

We had Jaycee members each take four or five of the youngsters to the stores in town to let them do their Christmas shopping. To show you how times have changed, we gave each of them five dollars.

One of the things we thought we might have to do is to explain to the children how to do their shopping and make sure they got the most for their money. We also thought we would need to give them some guidance selecting presents, if they were interested in getting gifts for other people.

It didn't take me long to learn that really wasn't going to be necessary at all. In fact, it was amazing to us to see how they stretched that five dollars.

I had four little boys in my group, ages seven and eight. I took them into the first store, which happened to be a JC Penney store, and I just followed them. They weren't interested in buying anything at all for themselves. What they really were looking for was something for someone else back at the orphanage, perhaps a little brother or sister or maybe the bus driver who always took them places or possibly one of the teachers.

I would have thought they might want to buy themselves a baseball glove or maybe a bat, all of which could be purchased at that time for five dollars, but that was not the case. As the youngsters went into the stores, the merchants also got into the Spirit of Giving by providing the children with lots of things for which they did not need to use any of their five dollars.

After about three hours of shopping in various stores, we were finished. At that time I said to my four boys, "We still have a little time. Why don't we go over to the drugstore and have a sundae?" Well, they thought that was a good idea, so I took them over to Myers' Drugstore in Hanover. We all sat up at the counter and had our sundaes.

After we were finished, we headed back to the school buses. At one of the street crossings on the way, there was a lady standing with the familiar bell and collection pot, clothed in a Salvation Army uniform. As we approached her, one of my little guys looked up at me and said, "Sir, I still have four nickels that I didn't spend. Would it be okay if I put them into that lady's pot over there?" I said, "Oh, that would be a very nice thing to do."

I watched him go over and drop his four nickels into that pot. And when he looked up at the lady and she looked down at him, there was something about the meeting of their eyes that we sometimes called a "Kodak moment." The smiles I saw on both of their faces were so touching.

Following that exchange, we made our way over to the bus. As this little boy got up on the running board, he turned around and looked at me at eye level and said, "God bless you, Mr. Gouker. This has been the happiest day of my life. I will never forget you." And then he ran to the back of the bus and took his seat.

I felt a lump in my throat that didn't permit me to answer him, but his words, and his little act of kindness, reminded me of the real meaning of Christmas.

History of "Letters to Santa"

When I came back from the service as a young man, I really did not know what I wanted to do with the rest of my life. Nevertheless, I accepted a position at the post office in Hanover, Pennsylvania.

While working long hours at Christmastime, I could not help but notice the volume of letters addressed to Santa Claus. Aside from rare exceptions, these letters were thrown into the wastebasket. To me, that just wasn't right. These children were pouring out their hearts to the one person they thought could satisfy all of their wishes. It was my belief that someone should be answering those letters. And so, with the permission of the Hanover postmaster, Claude O. Meckley, I began doing just that.

With the help of Mack Messenger at the local print shop, I became equipped with Santa Claus stationery and envelopes. I enlisted my wife, Mary Louise, to help me answer the letters and I set up some ground rules. We would write at least a page and a half and we would answer every question the child asked. We would not promise children anything. Rather, we would lose them in conversation. We would talk about what was happening at the North Pole because that's what they really wanted to know anyway. To this day, that is still what they want to know.

That first year, we answered 249 letters between December 11th and December 24th. Then, as time went on, we forgot about the letters. That is, until the following November. That's when it became apparent that the word was out that Santa Claus was answering his mail. The letters were not just coming from Hanover anymore. They were coming from all of the nearby towns and the neighboring state of Maryland. That year, we answered 569 letters!

Answering the children's letters quickly became a labor of love, which continues to this day. I have a strong belief that things happen for a reason. The fact that I was offered, and accepted, a position at the post office could not have been accidental. Had I not taken that job, I would not have been fortunate enough to enjoy 58 years of answering children's letters to Santa Claus.

For the first 47 years, I spent the hours I wasn't working banging out letters until the wee hours of the morning on a Royal portable manual typewriter. Despite my passion for the project, I realized I needed the help of even more of my family members, as the volume of letters increased each year.

That's where my daughters came in. When Patti, who was age five at the time I began this project, began asking why I had letters to Santa Claus lying all over the dining room table, I had to think fast to avoid spoiling her fun. So I simply told Patti, "You are so lucky because your dad has been asked to take care of the mail for Santa because he has so much to do. And I'm sure he would like it if you helped by putting stamps on the letters." Patti not only accepted that explanation, she also became my helper.

A while later, Peggy came along and also helped with the stamps; however, as time went on, both girls learned the truth about their dad as Santa Claus. Eventually, it became apparent to me that Peggy was gifted at answering letters. During one Christmas season, when I was up to my ears in letters, I called Peggy over and told her Santa needed a break. I asked her to take over and just write a paragraph about the Brownies.

She typed, "The Brownies are having a great time up here with their snow bowling. They line up icicles for pins and then roll snowballs, trying to knock them over." It was then that I knew I had a real-life Brownie correspondent helper.

Her flair for answering letters continues to this day. When I moved to Lancaster, Peg took over answering all of the letters that were dropped off in the box on the cabin on Center Square in Hanover.

For the past eight years, my wife, Gloria, has helped me immensely by typing my dictated letters so I can focus completely on the creativity of developing and customizing each letter. I am now able to sit back and let my imagination run wild without having to also focus on the typing. I have often said, "I don't know what I would do without her." She polishes off the letters by adding stickers, Rudolph's signature, or a recipe from Mrs. Santa. She loves to add that personal touch. Gloria has become the real Mrs. Santa and is quite capable of answering letters, too, when I become overwhelmed.

I have always dreamed of writing a book about this project because I am so passionate about it, but I was never able to take the time out of my busy schedule to sit down and do it. When I was forced to slow down a few years ago, after I fell and lost the vision in my left eye and then faced a battle with macular degeneration, I decided to give it a try. I realized I might have been put in this position so I could realize my dream.

I have often said, "The only thing I haven't accomplished yet in my life is writing a book about my Santa Claus project." Well, here I am—at age 86—completing the only goal I had ever set and not achieved.

How do you get down my chimney?

Why do you like to eat lots of cookies?

Do you give people shirts for Christmas?

Where do the elves come from?

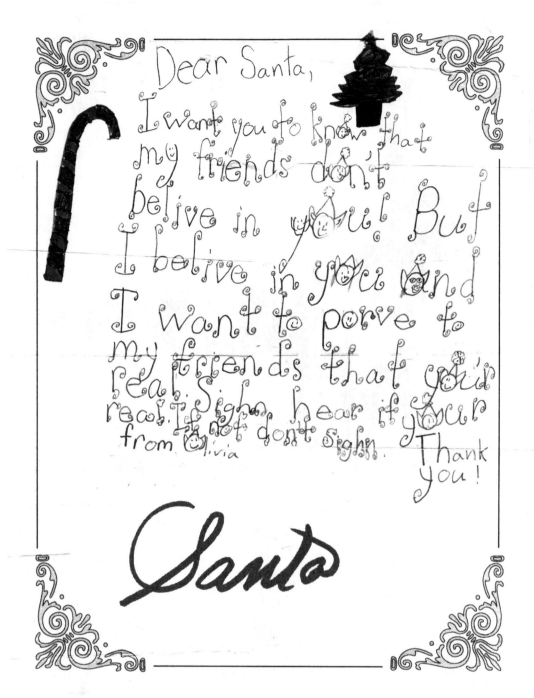

"*Dear Santa,*
I want you to know that my friends don't belive in you! But I belive in you and I want to porve to my friends that you'r real. Sign hear if your real. If not don't sign. Thank you!
from, Olivia"

Mrs. Santa Claus

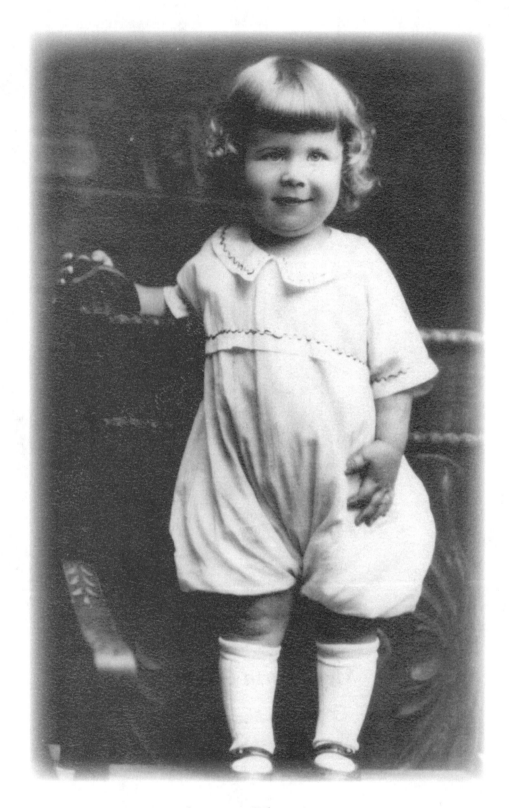

Santa Claus